# On God, The Soul, Evil and the Rise of Christianity

# READING AUGUSTINE

Series Editor: Miles Hollingworth

*Reading Augustine* offers personal and close readings of St Augustine of Hippo from leading philosophers and religious scholars. Its aim is to make clear Augustine's importance to contemporary thought and to present Augustine not only or primarily as a pre-eminent Christian thinker but as a philosophical, spiritual, literary and intellectual icon of the West.

## VOLUMES IN THE SERIES:

# On God, The Soul, Evil and the Rise of Christianity

*John Peter Kenney*

BLOOMSBURY ACADEMIC
NEW YORK • LONDON • OXFORD • NEW DELHI • SYDNEY

BLOOMSBURY ACADEMIC
Bloomsbury Publishing Inc
1385 Broadway, New York, NY 10018, USA
50 Bedford Square, London, WC1B 3DP, UK

BLOOMSBURY, BLOOMSBURY ACADEMIC and the Diana logo are trademarks
of Bloomsbury Publishing Plc

First published in the United States of America 2019

Cover design: Catherine Wood
Cover image © Mike Hill / Getty Images

A catalog record for this book is available from the Library of Congress.

ISBN: HB: 978-1-5013-1399-8
PB: 978-1-5013-1398-1
ePDF: 978-1-5013-1401-8
eBook: 978-1-5013-1400-1

Series: Reading Augustine

Typeset by Deanta Global Publishing Services, Chennai, India
Printed and bound in the United States of America

To find out more about our authors and books visit www.bloomsbury.com and
sign up for our newsletters.

*For madeline and tim, ted and maura*

# CONTENTS

# PREFACE

Some time ago, at the end of the 1960s, I set out to think through the idea of God. This book is a report on what I discovered. After surveying contemporary philosophy of religion, I decided to turn back to the ancient founders of philosophical monotheism, to the thinkers who first articulated the concept of God. I wanted to read their treatises in the original languages, interrogate their ideas and understand their accounts of reality. And so I began tracing the emergence of monotheism in late antiquity, for it was then that Pagan, Jewish and Christian thinkers hammered out the Western conception of God. Among those who did that hard thinking was a North African rhetorician and convert to Catholic Christianity who became known through history as Saint Augustine. It was his understanding of God that became central to the God of Latin Christianity. Amid his struggle to accept the God of Christian orthodoxy, Augustine wrote an autobiography – perhaps the first such work – that offered an insider's guide to the Christian belief in one God. That work, the *Confessions,* explains how and why Augustine had come around to this belief after many years of personal turmoil and doubt.

Augustine proved to be an indispensable source for my project of retrieving and assessing ancient monotheism, in this case in its Christian form. In reading him I was startled, over and over again, by unexpected aspects of his account of the Christian God, by ideas unfamiliar to me. Those ideas nested in a larger representation of the texture of reality and in spiritual practices that knit the fabric of his Christian account of God together. All this seemed strikingly distinctive and far removed from much contemporary thinking about God, both in philosophy and theology. That sense of distance catalysed the writing of this book. Following Augustine, I propose to explore the special character of the God of ancient Christianity as it appeared to its most brilliant Latin exponent. What follows will not be a study of monotheism as an abstract philosophical idea, but of that belief as it took shape within Christianity. For that too is something I discovered – that theoretical accounts neglect vital elements of religious belief, draining the force and meaning from ideas that exist within human life. Thus, understanding belief in one God requires careful and detailed reflection on a specific religious trajectory. But nonetheless, as we shall see, the study of Augustine's theology can only be accomplished by reference to other religious traditions and sources, for those traditions are permeable and develop by assimilation. That was particularly true in the late Roman Empire, a protean age when an array of religious groups with sharply conflicting theologies were competing for adherents. So, while the primary focus here will be on Augustine and the God of classical Christianity, the wider variety of ancient theologies will remain in view.

This book is for anyone who has wondered about the emergence of the God of the ancient Christians. It is meant for inquiring minds, including students, scholars and readers intrigued by ancient Christian philosophy and theology. I have wanted to write this book for some years in order to reflect on this subject in a fashion accessible beyond the confines of the academy. I am grateful to Miles Hollingworth and Bloomsbury for the invitation to do so. Over the years I have written monographs and studies on the subjects treated here. Those who would like to read more detailed discussions might wish to consult them; they are listed in the bibliography. In keeping with the intended audience, I have embedded scholarly references within the text and a list of those works can also be found in the bibliography. The works of Augustine and other ancient authors mentioned in the text are there as well. Because Augustine's *Confessions* is central to the topics treated in this book, the reader is encouraged to read the original. There are many fine editions in English available. Since it is important to capture the voice and texture of Augustine's prose, I have included substantial quotations. Translations of texts from Latin and Greek within the body of the text are my own. Finally, the reader should be alert to the fact that the term 'Christianity' has generally been used to refer to the mainstream orthodox tradition that Augustine espoused. But 'Christianity' was a diverse phenomenon in antiquity and I have indicated when that more capacious meaning of the term is intended.

This project would never have been produced without an academic squad of supporters. I have profited greatly from conversations with many scholars, especially Douglas Hedley of Cambridge, Paul Kolbet of Yale and my present and former Saint Michael's colleagues Carol and Ronald Begley, James Byrne, John Izzi, Raymond Patterson and Jeanne-Nicole Mellon Saint-Laurent. The late William Harmless S. J., of blessed memory, was especially important to the development of my work and his untimely death has been a profound loss. I wish to express my thanks to the president and trustees of Saint Michael's College for granting me a timely sabbatical leave in the autumn of 2016. My wife Ann has been, as always, a sustaining presence in my life and work, and I am profoundly grateful to her. And our children and their spouses have taken on an active advisory role, reminding me that this is a book meant to include readers of their generation. So it is dedicated to them: Madeline and Tim, Ted and Maura.

November 2017
Saint Michael's College
Vermont, USA

# Introduction:

# Reading Augustine

This is an essay on transcendence. It concerns a level of reality beyond space and time and materiality, and probes the emergence of this arresting notion in late antiquity. Moreover, it is a study in the salience of Christianity as understood through the mind of its greatest ancient interpreter, Augustine of Hippo. He tells us about his experiences of transcendence in a spiritual autobiography, the *Confessions*. There he recounts the transformative impact of those moments of Christian enlightenment and why he came to see Christ as the guarantor of eternal life for his soul. The privileged access of the *Confessions* allows us to see from within the conceptual shape of ancient Christianity, and to grasp why it seemed so compelling to Augustine. That is why reading Augustine is now imperative. It offers us a chance to discover why he regarded Christianity as a portal into the hidden but ineluctable presence of God within the innermost recesses of the human soul.

It is only when we read Augustine as a stranger that we can begin to understand him. Any other approach means seeing him through the prism of someone else's ideas. In some measure it is his cultural familiarity that separates us from him, since each adoption of his ideas through the centuries has retrieved Augustine at the partial expense of his own thought. Yet because his influence was so pervasive, it is difficult to disaggregate Augustine from the myriad forms of Augustinianism. Some of these appropriations seem fruitful and worth their reshaping the original; others seem distortive and even perverse. But it is also possible to read Augustine in the context of his own world, surrounding his thought with the texts that he read and the ideas that he says were influential to him. That will be the approach here in this study, to read Augustine himself and follow the trail of his thought. And that can be quite startling at times. While many of Augustine's ideas form the received categories of Western Christianity, some striking aspects of his thinking have fallen out of solution. So the goal in this volume is thus to look more closely at the patterns of Augustine's thinking itself, with an eye to his interlocutors and the influences that he acknowledged. It must be admitted that contextualization of this sort is itself a hermeneutical practice, dependent on the selection of ancient sources chosen as the framework for interpretation. But it is, at least, a strategy that begins by coming to grips with the ancient texts themselves, and builds directly upon them, sifting them with a focus on their internal logic and their external conceptual environment. This style of reading a figure like Augustine also holds the promise that, by carefully examining the distant concepts of the ancient world, we can then sharpen our own responses to the perennial questions that we share with the ancients.

When Augustine resolved to be baptized as a Catholic Christian, he said that there were two things he wanted to learn about: God and the soul (*Soliloquies* 2.7). Nothing more. And that is what we shall be doing along with him, tracing what he says he came to know, and then sifting through the inner logic of his new Christian philosophy. But as we get started, we should admit that his was a strange story, when viewed from our distant vantage point. There are several reasons why this is so. First, it is common to think that Augustine converted from some sort of pagan polytheism to Christianity. But that's not what happened. In fact, Augustine was some sort of Christian during his whole life, sometimes only a nominal Catholic catechumen, sometimes a passionate advocate of Manichaeism, a sectarian form of Christianity, and later a Catholic monk and bishop, but nonetheless a Christian throughout. That fact should alert us to a crucial but popularly neglected aspect of the ancient Christian world: it was a big tent encompassing many sects and varieties. So Augustine's trajectory was Christian, describing an arc across the firmament of early Christianity.

Yet he was also powerfully influenced by paganism – not by its polytheistic cults, towards which he never shows any sympathy, but by its philosophical schools. For Augustine was trained as a rhetorician, and his classical education in the liberal arts and in the practice of rhetoric meant that he became familiar with the teachings of the most notable philosophers. He never joined a philosophical school and was thus never formally instructed in doctrine and ethical practices under the supervision of a teacher. But he nonetheless acquired an outsider's grasp of the major philosophies of the late antique world. Here we need to take special notice of the fact that many ancient philosophers were not just engaged in conceptual problem-solving, though they did plenty of that, but more importantly they taught specific ethical precepts that adherents were expected to follow. Learning how to live in the hard world of antiquity was the purpose of philosophy, and the wisdom it promised was meant to be conducive to a happy life. Philosophy in antiquity was, therefore, not an armchair discipline, but 'a way of life', something to which you fully committed yourself (Hadot, 1995). That meant that you were introduced to an account of reality by a teacher and trained through discussion in the doctrines of that school. Those became your moral blueprint, something that you practised with the aid of meditative techniques and ascetical discipline. These philosophies nested in the large and amorphous world of traditional paganism, sometimes in creative tension with its religious myths about the gods, sometimes creatively engaged with them. So for us to understand the significance of philosophy to Augustine, we need to bear all this in mind and enlarge our sense of the meaning and scope of the term.

This recognition should help make sense of the puzzle of Augustine's religious trajectory. Augustine was born in 354 into a North African family divided along religious lines: his father Patricius was a religiously indifferent pagan and his mother Monica was a devout Catholic. When Augustine became old enough to make his own religious choice, he opted for neither. Instead he became a Manichee, a legally proscribed and secretive sect that claimed to be the true and most rational form of Christianity. It was one of dozens of groups that scholars loosely classify as 'gnostic' forms of Christianity, because of their rejection of the Old Testament and their emphasis on salvation through knowledge – in Greek *gnosis* (King 2005). Then, after about a decade, Augustine soured on it, coming to regard its claims of esoteric knowledge to be at odds with his studies in the classical sciences. After a period of sceptical uncertainty, during which he signed up as a Catholic catechumen in order to advance his career, he began to read Platonism seriously. Some Catholic intellectuals seem to have put him on to philosophical treatises from the Roman Platonic school. That dose of pagan philosophy catalysed a deep and power reorientation, leading him to convert not only to Catholic Christianity but also to an ascetical and philosophical way of life.

Now it must be admitted that this story, on the face of it, makes little sense, especially at our distance across the centuries. It is an odd tale that zigzags from one form of Christianity to another via pagan philosophy. As it happens, Augustine's story required an explanation in his own time as well, and thus we have his narration of how all this worked out, the *Confessions*. The privileged access provided by that work allows us to see into the ambient religious currents beneath the surface of the tale itself. And thereby we can come to a better perspective on why an intellectual-like Augustine would have found orthodox Christianity so compelling. Moreover, Augustine's self-articulated narrative helps us to grasp the menu of religious options that were live in late antiquity. And that too allows us to discern and assess the slow shift towards monotheism that was occurring across the Roman Empire. So the complexity and occasional opacity of Augustine's story are boons to us, supplying an unrivalled sense of the religious vitality of his age and an inner description of theological options that might otherwise seem remote and even bizarre.

The plan of this book will follow Augustine's path. We will begin Chapter 1 by discussing what were central questions for Augustine: How do we know that there is one God, and how do we know the nature of that God? To that end we'll need to look closely at a series of episodes that Augustine describes in the central books of the *Confessions*. To understand them we'll need to retrace his antecedent religious and philosophical commitments. In particular, ancient dualism – the belief in two distinct powers at the base of reality – calls for some reflection. Along with dualism, we'll also have to follow Augustine's struggle with materialism, the understanding that all reality is physical and is bound by the cosmos. A version of that theory is, of course, still with us as the cornerstone of scientific naturalism, so Augustine's efforts to overcome this representation of reality bear directly on the debates of our own time.

What freed Augustine from dualism and materialism, and opened the path to Catholicism, was Platonism. That move will require careful consideration to sort out. But suffice it to say that

Platonism had two key elements that were critical to Augustine. By late antiquity, Platonism was a form of monotheism, accepting an ultimate first principle, the One or Good, at the core of reality. It was, therefore, opposed to dualism. Indeed, the Platonists of Augustine's time had struggled hard to overcome classical dualism. Hence the initial appeal of Platonism to someone like Augustine, who was trying to move beyond Manichaean dualism. Moreover, Platonism offered Augustine a philosophically nuanced account of a level reality beyond matter and the physical cosmos. That was the spiritual heart of Platonism, the existence of a perfect reality from which our world of pain and confusion had emerged and to which our souls might aspire to return. This theory – which we might call 'transcendentalism' – maintained, therefore, that there exists a higher level of reality beyond space and time. This Platonic account of transcendence was the most powerful antidote to materialism in antiquity. Indeed, it has continued in that role down through the centuries of Western philosophy until the present day (Gerson, 2017). Augustine tells us that when he encountered the idea of transcendence, he had never really understood it before, but when he did, everything changed for him. His reading of Platonism catalysed the conversionary experiences just alluded to moments of immediate knowledge of God. Unpacking and reflecting on those will be the final focus of Chapter 1.

Chapter 2 will take us into the larger implications of Augustine's new theology. We will need to spend some time considering this quite arresting notion of a transcendent God and the means necessary to discern him. For Augustine says that he came to know God not as a theoretical object, nor as a distinct person, nor as a separate thing, but as something that radically resists finite representation. This knowledge exposed his soul's total dependence on God for his existence. Thus, he did not know about God, rather his soul came directly into the divine presence. That sort of thinking makes descriptions of God seem largely beside the point. And indeed, that is what Augustine came to believe: that knowledge about God is not a matter of theory and analysis, of description and conceptual representation. For he says he had immediate knowledge of God in the depth of his self. Augustine's Platonist sources called this kind of knowledge 'contemplation'. It was understood to be the result of the innermost soul's capacity to stretch beyond the material realm and achieve transcendent association with the divine. To get at it, we'll need to shed our accustomed forms of analytic reflection and to grasp how this deep power in the soul offers the promise of transcendence through contemplation. Doing so will lead us to realize how different Augustine's thinking is from our own, including from much contemporary Christian theology.

What will also become clear is how seriously Augustine took this radical new perspective on reality. To know God requires reorientation of the whole self, not just an exercise of the mind. This too Augustine learned from the Platonists. Their understanding of the philosophical life called for an intense change in the moral character of the self, an inner spiritual renewal, leading to the soul's recovery of its inherently divine condition. That restoration of the soul's divinity was the goal of Platonism, and philosophy was the path to it. Through philosophy, the highest, rational part of the soul could connect again to the transcendent level of reality from which it had departed and to which it longed to return. All these ideas fit coherently around the core Platonic understanding of transcendence. Augustine soon grasped the shape and force of Platonic philosophy, yet he insisted that he could not follow it. But the fault was not his. Generalizing from his own experience, he came to regard the Platonic account of the soul, and its latent divine power, to be overblown. It was, in his estimation at least, an inhuman representation of human nature.

Augustine wrote his own story in the *Confessions* in part to make that point. In effect, he invited his readers to consider his life, and then their own, and to decide whether they thought that the human soul was divine and capable of spiritual self-restoration. For his part, he knew the answer. Human beings might aspire to moral tranquillity and may hope to achieve transcendence of this world, but we don't have that power latent within. Chapter 3 will, therefore, require us to look closely at his alternative Christian account of the soul. Here the necessity of divine assistance in the reorientation of the soul towards the transcendent comes to the fore. That need relates to Augustine's assessment of the soul's fall from its original state of perfection and the need for divine grace. The interiority of contemplation disclosed not just access to a higher world, but also what lies deep within the dark recesses of the soul. No account of Augustine can neglect his bracing inventory of that darkness within and his understanding of the spiritual poverty of the human soul.

Mention of the fall takes us into the topic of Chapter 4: evil. In our contemporary discussions of religion, evil is frequently regarded as a primary theoretical impediment to belief in God. But this was not the case for ancient monotheists such as Augustine. To understand his conversion to orthodox Christianity, we need to follow his developing accounts of evil. In his narratives of contemplative union, Augustine indicates that to know God is to know evil as well. For contemplation throws the state of the human soul into relief over against the infinite goodness of God. By coming to know God contemplatively, the soul comes into the presence of the divine – lifted up, Augustine says, by the power of the Spirit. It is in a state of anticipatory realization of what the afterlife of purified souls is like. That moment of complete understanding, as he calls it, floods the soul with the infinite goodness that is God. And then the soul falls away to its earthly life, embedded as it is in sin. In that moment the soul comes to recognize its complicity in evil. To know God is also to disclose to the soul its distance from God. That separation is the product of the fall, the soul's inherent turn into itself and away from God. It is what it now is, not because it was created in its present condition, but because it chose something over God. And what it chose was itself. The root of sin is pride, that is, self-orientation and the love of self. But only God can restore the soul to its original state of communion with himself. Augustine came to see that Christianity had the solution to the problem of evil, one that was not simply a theoretical answer. It was through Christ's incarnation and death that humanity was offered the power to overcome the power of sin and death. Christ alone overcame death and only through his power can the human soul do so as well.

So on Augustine's account, the pagan Platonism had misunderstood the human condition, overestimating the power of the soul and underestimating the depth of the fall. Only orthodox Christianity had an adequate account of human nature, and crucially offered access to the power needed for us to recover. Hence Augustine's Christianity is a radical departure from classical philosophy. It is this salience – the rise of Christianity as a distinctive account of reality – that is the focus of the concluding Chapter 5. There we will consider the features of orthodox Christianity that made it stand out to Augustine as particularly compelling. Chief among these is the Catholic insistence that the incarnation of Christ was intended to confer divinity on the human soul. 'God became human so that humans could become divine.' That slogan may not sound like Christian orthodoxy to contemporary ears, but it was the core credendum of Augustine's new religion. We will need to take account of the striking level of intimacy between the soul and God that Augustine's theology proposed. As a religion of communion, that relation between God and the soul was effected by the power of the 'whole Christ', both the Christ transcendent of his creation, and the salvific Christ immanent in his church. That confronts us with the deep synergy that Augustine discovered in another Catholic teaching, the communion of saints. This he understood as describing the spiritual connection across the bounds of materiality among embodied human souls within the church, the souls of the heavenly Jerusalem, and Christ their head. These powerful metaphysical teaching secured for Christianity a novel account of God and the soul, the things Augustine had set out to grasp at the time of his conversion. If we have followed him this far, we will have done enough.

# 1

# Christian Enlightenment

*And I heard as one hears in the heart, and from that moment there was no longer any doubt.*

Augustine came to believe in the God of orthodox Christianity because he had no choice. He tells us in his *Confessions* that sometime around 384, when he was in a sceptical mood, he was completely overwhelmed by the presence of God, so much so that it would have been easier to doubt that he existed, than to doubt the reality of God (*Confessions* VII.10.16). This moment of understanding secured for him personal certainty about the existence of God and catalysed a new departure in his spiritual life.

We have all heard stories like this before: Prince Gautama's enlightenment beneath the bodhi tree in Bodh Gaya, or the rabbi Saul's blinding encounter with the risen Christ on the road to Damascus, his soul caught up to the third heaven. Lives forever changed; new spiritual movements initiated. So it was with Augustine. At the height of his fame as a rhetorician at the Imperial Roman Court, several moments of enlightenment led him not only to become a Catholic Christian but to abandon his worldly life and adopt asceticism. Before his enlightenment he had written only a short treatise, afterwards he generated hundreds of books, treatises, sermons and letters – over five million words. He had been transformed by the God of the Christians.

This chapter explores how Augustine found his way into orthodox Christianity through this transformative experience. But he was the first to admit that this outcome was initially unlikely. To understand why this was so, and what was going on in this momentous transition, we need first to consider his religious trajectory. That will then allow us to consider what options he rejected as he moved towards Christian monotheism and why he finally embraced it.

# Varieties of Christianity

Augustine lived in an age that was not short on religious options. This was true not only of the Roman Empire as a whole, but also of his home province of Africa. Born in 354 in what is now Algeria, he grew up inland about 60 miles from the Mediterranean. His father Patricius was a successful farmer, with some regional significance as a member of the local Roman governing class. Patricius was a pagan, and an indifferent one at that. Augustine offers a brief but harsh portrait of him in the *Confessions*. He sketches him as a man without moral bearings and fiercely determined to improve his family's status by advancing his son's career as a rhetorician. Patricius eventually converted to Catholicism near the end of his life. By contrast his mother Monica was a committed Catholic, yet she too emerges from his autobiography as ambitious for her son. In her case, those ambitions were not entirely worldly, but included her intention to see Augustine baptized as a Catholic. She stalked him throughout his adult career, following him when he moved from Carthage to Rome and finally to Milan as he advanced in his profession.

Although Monica was keen to see her son become a Catholic, she did not have him baptized as an infant, a practice that was beginning to take hold in the period. Instead she delayed, Augustine tells us, because she wanted to wait until the moral storms of his adolescence had passed. The depiction of his adolescence in the *Confessions* suggests she may have had a point. If baptism was the one certain means for the remission of sin, better to hold off until maturity. But Augustine was almost baptized when his life seemed endangered by a fever, but the moment passed. Monica did have him enrolled as a Catholic catechumen, so that he was introduced to the basic teachings of his mother's religion from his youth. Later on, after his conversion to orthodoxy, he would remember this fact fondly, recounting to a childhood friend how Catholicism had been grafted into his sinews from his youth (*Against the Academics* 2.2.5).

So it is fair to say that Augustine was brought up and educated within the ambience of orthodox Christianity, even if he was never formally admitted through baptism.

Yet the Catholicism that Monica followed was by no means the largest Christian body in North Africa. In fact, Donatist Christianity was the dominant group in Augustine's youth. The Donatists were a Christian sect whose theology was largely the same as the Catholics, except that they refused to countenance the readmission of Christians who had submitted to the Roman government and forsworn their Christian faith during the final worldwide persecution in 303–13 initiated under the pagan Emperor Diocletian. This was an acute matter in the case of clergy who had avoided torture and death by offering sacrifice to the pagan gods or surrendered the Gospel books for burning by Roman authorities. Should they simply be allowed to resume their roles, or was rebaptism and reconsecration necessary? Were the sacramental rituals that they had performed even valid? Naturally enough, there had been a wide range of accommodative behaviour, some of it designed to fool Roman authorities by surrendering non-canonical texts. Many Christians of all backgrounds had avoided persecution by slipping out of town until things blew over.

After the practice of Christianity became legal in 313, what to do with Christians who had committed various levels of apostasy became an exigent question. The followers of Donatus, a claimant to the episcopal office in Carthage, insisted on rigorism. Those Christians, whether lay or clerical, who had apostatized in any way before the Roman authorities would need to do penance and be rebaptized. Moreover, the sacraments performed by those apostate clergy were regarded as null and void, tainted by the sin of faithless clergy who had exercised their clerical office in an impaired moral state. In contrast, the Catholics required only acts of contrition and penance in order for apostates to be reinstated, not rebaptism. In the case of apostate clergy, they regarded the efficacy of the sacraments they had performed to be independent of the moral state of the officiating clergy. On the ground in North Africa, the rigorism of the Donatists won out, perhaps because the issues involved were more than just religious, but included political attitudes towards Roman imperial control in North Africa. Indeed, radical Donatists, known as Circumcellions, engaged in a military insurgency in opposition to Roman rule. After Augustine became a Catholic bishop, it appears that Circumcellions attempted to assassinate him several times. But the Donatists were prone to internal divisions and were eventually suppressed by Roman authorities in the early fifth century; their churches were surrendered to the imperially sanctioned Catholics and their adherents encouraged to rejoin. Augustine would acquiesce to this act of religious coercion, in large measure because of his estimation of the tacitly political character of the conflict and the sporadic violence that it had engendered. Scholars continue to assess his motives and complicity in this act of suppression (Brown 2000).

The nature of this division among North African Christians should alert us to the position of Catholic Christianity and its eventual appeal to Augustine. For Catholicism was the branch of Christianity that maintained the orthodox definition of Christianity decided at the Council of Nicaea in 324–5, the first worldwide council of bishops after legalization. This Nicene Christianity understood itself to be Catholic or universal, emerging from several centuries of discussion over the uniqueness of the One God and the nature of Jesus Christ. That process was perforce an internal one while the Christian movement was illegal, but it surfaced into the imperial sunlight when Constantine called the bishops to Nicaea. It was on that public stage that the Catholic Church was now required to settle exactly what it believed about Christ and his relation to the God of the Hebrew scriptures. Out of that critical moment of religious self-definition emerged Catholic monotheism.

The creed that was cobbled together tells us much about the disputed issues within the Christian mainstream and leaves a great deal under-defined. It begins most importantly by establishing the divine Father as the centre of monotheism and its does so by characterizing him as the 'maker of heaven and earth'. The Son of God is described as 'only begotten' from the Father. There is a clear imperative to make the connection between these two as tight as possible, with the Son's derivation presented as 'from the substance of the Father', as 'God from God', as 'light from light' and as 'true God from true God'. The Son is 'begotten not made, of one substance with the Father'. It is also that 'through whom all things came into being, things in heaven and on earth'. So the logic of Nicene monotheism is based on the essential connection of Father to Son, and on the sharp line of demarcation between what is uncreated and what is created. That formula throws into relief the inner nature of God shared by the Father and Son, and it brings to the fore the idea of divine creation as the bright seam of separation between God and everything else. This would one day become the creed of Augustine, although only later in his life, and only after he was able to interpret its sketchy language with greater philosophical precision.

It bears mention that while the council settled on this theology, it threw into relief other widely held theological views within the Christian movement. The creed of Nicaea came attached with a set of rejected ideas that help us see beneath the surface of its assertions and into the minds of its opponents. The 'Holy, Catholic, and Apostolic Church' anathematized any suggestion that the Son is of a different substance from the Father, or that the Son is created, or that the Son could undergo alteration or change. Underlying those claims was a version of Christian monotheism associated with Arius, an Alexandrian presbyter. Although the ideas he espoused had been debated long before the council, the powerful faction at the council which adopted them became known to history as Arians. That form of Christian theism regarded the Father as the true God and placed the Son on the other side of the line of creation. The 'first-born of all creation' is a Pauline phrase from Col. 1.15. Arians interpreted it to mean that only the Father was uncreated. Thus, the Son must be of a different nature from the Father and, like all mundane things, the Son must be subject to change. This Arian theology had several appealing aspects. It made it easy to envision the person and mission of Jesus Christ, seen as an intermediary power whose incarnation was consistent with his inherent nature as a creature. It also made Christianity a form of monotheism straightforwardly continuous with the religion of ancient Israel, since this was an exclusive monotheism that understood the oneness of God in a strictly numerical fashion. Indeed, its persuasive force was sufficient to keep Arianism popular and under continuous debate throughout Augustine's lifetime. Members of the imperial family shifted back and forth between Nicene and Arian Christianity for decades. Moreover, the barbarian Visigoths who sacked Rome in 410 were Arians, converted by exiled Arian missionaries. As Augustine lay dying in 430, Hippo Regius, the city where he had preached Catholicism for decades, was besieged by the Vandals. In a bitter irony, they too were Arians.

These were some of the more dominant forms of Christianity in the age of Augustine. Yet, when he reached his late adolescence and went to study the liberal arts in Carthage, Augustine chose a very different path. He was drawn into a proscribed sort of Christianity, Manichaeism. Strikingly, Manichaeism was not even a form of monotheism, yet it had an appeal to Augustine that Nicene Catholicism lacked. That was its claim to intellectual sophistication. Looking back when he wrote his *Confessions*, Augustine tells us that the Manichees he encountered during his days as a student in Carthage presented their theology as rational and scientific. In contrast, the Catholicism of his rural childhood seemed to him deficient intellectually. In particular, the Manichees rejected as ridiculous the God of the Old Testament, a God depicted in anthropomorphic terms, with hands, feet and unpredictable mood swings. The hometown Catholicism of Augustine's North African youth evidently took a largely literalist approach to the reading of scripture.

Before we follow him into Manichaeism, it is worth taking a moment to recognize the significance of this point. When he wrote his autobiography, Augustine was a newly consecrated Catholic bishop. Part of his motivation in telling his story lay in the need to explain his complicated religious past. It was awkward enough to have been a Manichee for a decade or so. But worse was the fact that he had started out as a Catholic catechumen in his youth but had rejected his mother's religion. In the *Confessions* he is quite explicit that his reason was intellectual. He had failed to discover a concept of God that he regarded as adequate or defensible, a God free from naïve anthropomorphism. That failure was driven by the literalistic biblicism of his hometown Catholicism, as well as by its lack of philosophical articulation. He says that he was never able to imagine a God who was not in some sense physical, even if that God was understood as the maker of things visible and invisible. So what the young Augustine required from Catholicism was more than the God he had encountered in the Nicene Creed and the Bible. And so he drifted off elsewhere. It would take him many years before he finally found what had been missing in his first exposure to Catholicism.

Where he went was to an esoteric form of Christianity founded by Mani, a Persian who styled himself as the 'apostle of Jesus Christ'. While things ended badly for him, with his crucifixion by the Persian government in 276, the sect he founded survived by spreading both into the Roman Empire and out into the East. It travelled along the Silk Road all the way to China and beyond in the medieval period. So it was a force to be reckoned with, one whose inherent religious character was sufficiently compelling to draw significant adherents across many different cultures. Some of its teachings might, it is fair to say, strike contemporary readers as bizarre, as they ultimately came to seem to Augustine. But the outline of its main theological teaching is what interests us. What is most striking about Manichaeism is not just its postulation of two primordial powers, but in particular its presentation of these forces as locked in struggle with one another. This is the most salient aspect of Manichaeism. It is what might be called a 'conflict dualism'; that is, it centres on the cosmic battle between two powers whose enmity defines the nature of reality.

Dualism was a ubiquitous cosmology in antiquity. Versions can be found throughout the ancient philosophical schools. Most of those theories claimed that two primordial powers were responsible for the cosmos, yet they were compatible with each other, not in conflict. They were distinct poles united by their interaction. For example, Plato's great cosmological dialogue, the *Timaeus*, describes a primal power called 'space' that is full of discordant motion. It is the stuff used by a divine agent, the demiurge, to craft the cosmos, shaping it according to an independent divine pattern. The disorder of spatial chaos is said to yield to the persuasion of order, even if it remains recalcitrant to rational structure. Plato's story can be read to describe a continuous process with its own inherent logic, an account of two fundamental powers – order and disorder – that constitute the ingredients of reality. This pattern can be found as well in the thought of Plato's student Aristotle, who understood primordial matter as the potential foundation for the rational structure of the cosmos, drawn by the magnetism of divine order. So too the Stoics held a modified dualism, such that God or Nature encompassed the cosmos as an immanent power, but was itself divided into two poles. These were the active power of reason, the Logos, identified with fire, and the passive power of matter that is inert but receptive of rational ordering. Both powers permeate the cosmos.

All these ancient philosophical sorts of dualism, while postulating a principle separate from reason and order, nonetheless envisioned a comprehensive and rational pattern of association between the two poles. But this was not the case with Manichaeism. Instead, it presented these two powers as actively at odds and their cosmic struggle as intense and ongoing. The cosmos was thus not the best of all possible worlds that could have emerged from the confluence of two different sources, but the violent by-product of their ongoing clash. These two opposing principles were the power of goodness, light and spirit, over against the power of evil, darkness and matter. In Manichaeism the light was passive while evil was active, the ravenous power of the dark side. Moreover, these conflicting forces were not understood metaphorically, but were actual physical powers at odds within the visible cosmos. For that reason Manichaeism could present itself to postulants like Augustine as a scientific account of the natural universe, as much physics as metaphysics. And so for Manichees the battle between the immensity of darkness and the restricted points of goodness was writ large in the night sky. To Manichees, darkness was literally – nor figuratively – evil, and its ferocity could be directly seen by the naked eye in the war of the worlds above, as the bright goodness of meteors was extinguished by evil darkness and the planets occluded. The sun was the source of all goodness and light; the moon a halfway station for light particles who had escaped from bodies and were collecting themselves for the perilous journey back to the sun. We humans were venues for that cosmic struggle. Within those who were Manichees, there was a ruined fragment of primordial light, a spark of goodness, a bit of the divine spirit actually encased in the evil matter of the physical body. The goal of Manichees was passive resistance to the irrational passions that afflict the spirit, and the withdrawal of the spirit from the darkness that had physically covered over its true inner nature. Hence, rigorous asceticism was the norm for high-level Manichaean saints, the 'perfect ones', and something to be aspired to by 'hearers', the second-class members like Augustine who were still finding their way into the light within them.

Augustine was a Manichee for about a decade. Gradually, as his studies in the liberal arts progressed, he came to suspect that Manichaeism lacked the intellectual warrant that he had been led to believe. In particular he came to notice an obvious divergence between what the Manichees claimed about the nature of the cosmos and what he discovered in his reading of the classical physical sciences. He also grew to believe that Manichaean theories were in some cases quite implausible and ridiculous. A particularly striking instance of this was their belief that bits of divine light were trapped in fruit – a sort of theological version of photosynthesis. But those sparks could be released if the fruit were ingested and then vomited out by one of the Manichaean elect in an act of spiritual bulimia. Here is his description from *Confessions* III.10.18:

> Slowly, by stages, I was brought to believe nonsense; for example, that a fig weeps when picked, and the tree, its mother, weeps milky tears as well. However, if some saint were to eat a fig picked not by himself but by another, then he would mix it in his stomach and exhale angels, or more accurately, would belch out bits of God while groaning in prayer. These bits of the highest and true God would have been bound in that fruit unless they were saved by the tooth and belly of an elect saint. But miserable as I was, I believed that more mercy should be offered to the fruits of the earth than to human beings for whom they are grown. Yet if someone hungry, who was not a Manichee, asked for fruit, and I gave him some, then that piece would be seen as damned to capital punishment.

This vivid passage shows how deeply intertwined were theology and the physical sciences for the Manichees. Augustine came to realize that theories like this were not supported by the sort of rational analysis that his academic studies had led him to expect. In Book V of the *Confessions* those concerns are described as coming to a head when he finally met Faustus, the head of the Manichees, who failed to answer Augustine's probing questions.

Beyond these shortcomings was the character of Manichaean ethics, based on their special theory of human nature. This is hinted at in the passage above. Manichees regarded most humans as lacking a divine spark within them. That was reserved for Manichees. Most humans were by nature lacking in spiritual depth; hence, the dark fate of the light particle ingested by a non-Manichee. That elitism rankled Augustine. But there was another difficulty that went even deeper. Members of the Manichaean religion were understood to be divided into two sharply different, antagonistic natures: the spirit spark and the material body. The physical body literally encased the spirit in evil, obscuring its beneficent light in malevolent darkness.

The true self was thus immured in evil, so that the actions taken by Manichees in their earthly lives were really the result of passions residing in their bodies. Evil acts were thus not the product of the true self, but of the material envelope that presently surrounds them. Because the power of goodness and light was passive, the true self seemed not to be the source of human agency, but an impassive observer. In Augustine's view, this degraded any real sense of moral decision making, since the true self was, in fact, not the determent of human actions. Indeed, the passive, inner self seems just along for the ride. For Augustine, schooled in the classical Roman ethical tradition of Cicero, this came to be seen as a debilitating evasion of personal responsibility. It opened the door to deep sources of self-deception and alienation. Worse still, the Manichees deprecated moral struggle as a sign of spiritual inferiority. To struggle with the passions was to lack the inviolate light within, for moral struggle was the clearest token of fundamental depravity.

These shortcomings were significant to Augustine's eventual apostasy. But the deepest issue he had with Manichaeism lay in the nature of its metaphysics. Its dualism by definition precluded any final resolution for evil or any explanation for its very existence. Evil was elemental. It was a brute fact of reality, the dark side that would never go away. To a Manichee, evil was something that the spirit within must simply endure. Evil could be avoided, but it was never to be resolved into a higher good. Augustine's sustained analysis of this mode of theological thinking led him to identify the root of its failure in an inability to understand the true nature of reality. Manichaeism was a theology that, in a sense, recognized the destructive tension between good and evil, and left it at that. There was no deeper pattern beneath that surface struggle; there was just the struggle itself. To seek for its resolutions was to miss the point. But Augustine rejected that judgement. He came instead to regard such thinking as flawed in part because rationality is grounded in the search for reasons. And Manichaeism was content not to provide an ultimate answer to that most fundamental question: Why does the world exist? To him Manichaeism offered a penultimate response, a set of ingredients, but no ultimate explanation of their primordial origins.

The reason for that failure was Manichaeism's materialism. No meaning could be found for the existence of evil if there was nothing beyond the material plane into which evil could somehow be resolved. That is what Augustine came to recognize as the underlying problem with Manichaeism. Both good and evil were physical forces within the universe and there was nothing else deeper. The Good was, therefore, a finite material power. So Augustine was constrained to think of God as one pole in a cosmic battle against evil, 'a material substance with its own foul and misshapen mass' (*Confessions* V.10.20). Moreover, there was no underlying logic to this struggle, no tacit plan unfolding in the grim misery of earthly existence. It was this constriction of thought to materiality alone that was his false turn (*Confessions* V.10.19):

> And when I wished to think of my God, I did not know how to do so except as a physical mass. Nor did I think that something exists if it was not physical. And that was the greatest and almost sole cause of my inevitable error.

That is a strong claim. Materialism, as an encompassing theory about the nature of reality, leaves the fact of evil unexplained. It surrenders any account of evil's meaning; it acquiesces to evil's apparent place in the world; it concedes to evil an elemental place in reality. The only way beyond that stark admission was – in Augustine's view – to go deeper into the nature of reality, behind the manifest image of the world, and to discover the resolution of dualism in an ultimate God. To understand how that worked for him, we need to turn – surprisingly enough – to pagan philosophy.

## Pagan Monotheism

Sometime around 175, a pagan philosopher named Celsus was annoyed by a novel religious movement that rejected the traditional religion of the Empire. In response he wrote a polemical treatise to refute this new Christian movement entitled *True Doctrine*. We know some of his argument from excerpts found in a massive reply by Origen, the Christian philosopher (*Against Celsus* 8.12). Here's what he said:

> Now, if they worshipped only one God, one might fairly say that they have a straightforward claim against others. But in fact they excessively worship someone who appeared recently,

and nonetheless they do not think it is offensive to God if they worship his servant.

Let's stop and think about this for a moment. Here we have a pagan philosopher taking Christians to task for failing to be monotheists. It seems disconcerting to find this charge coming from a pagan, conditioned as we are to assume that paganism was entirely polytheistic. But this was evidently not the case. Celsus, a Platonist, regards himself as a monotheist. Yet somehow 'pagan monotheism' just doesn't sound right. We have a long-standing cultural disposition to regard monotheism as solely the product of ancient Israelite religion and to regard rabbinic Judaism and Christianity as its heirs. Conversely, we commonly regard Greco-Roman civilization as free from monotheism, with paganism understood as exclusively polytheistic. But that reading is not really accurate. Although Greco-Roman religion did indeed remain polytheistic in its cultic practices, there were also pronounced tendencies towards finding a divine source behind the complexities of the pantheon (Kenney 1986). By the time of Celsus, pagan monotheism had taken hold within a variety of different mystery cults and among the Platonic philosophical schools to which Celsus belonged (Kenney 1991; Athanassiadi and Frede 1999; Mitchell and van Nuffelen 2010).

This pagan monotheism was not borrowed from the Jews, and certainly not from the Christians, but had an indigenous logic all its own. Celsus makes that plain in his treatise against the Christians, *True Doctrine*. Notice that in the passage just cited, Celsus regards monotheism as a position consistent with reason. It is philosophically grounded and defensible. The problem with the Christians is their obsession with Jesus Christ whom they insist on elevating to the level of the great God. From Celsus's standpoint, this is violation of the logic of monotheism as pagans understood it. For Celsus, the one God is a source of lesser beings: the classical gods of the pantheon, intermediary beings like daemons, and humans. Those beings all represent aspects of the one God, focal manifestations of the rich reality of that ultimate divine being. So for Celsus the great God is one in an inclusive sense, as the deeper source of all that is good and beautiful within the lower ranks of beings dependent upon it. Thus, the great God is not so much one by exclusion of other gods, but one in the sense that it is the unity from which the many powers of the cosmos emerged. Notwithstanding his commitment to the existence of many lesser gods, Celsus can thus regard himself as a monotheist. Yet, he also rejects the Christian cult as failing to do justice to the richness of the one God, precisely because it fails to capture in its worship the myriad aspects of the One's fecundity. The practice of polytheistic worship is thus a requirement of pagan monotheism, not a violation of it. For Celsus, the many cults of Greco-Roman religion are, therefore, a natural and proper expression of true monotheism when understood in its inclusive sense. In the words of the pagan Platonist Symmachus, a contemporary of Augustine: 'Not by one path alone to so great a mystery' (*Memorial of Symmachus*).

Notwithstanding his commitment to monotheism, Celsus was in some measure a dualist. Like nearly all Platonists before the middle of the third century, he remained faithful to the cosmological model of Plato's *Timaeus*, mentioned above, in which the active agency of the great God, the demiurge, fashioned the cosmos by using some sort of underlying stuff. That substrate was a necessary condition of cosmic production and it was not the direct product of the one God. So at least in that sense, his was a finite theism, limited by something outside the one God that was necessary for divine production of the world. Although there was just one ultimate God, that great God was not alone sufficient to generate the cosmos. This model of limited monotheism would, however, be superseded in the next century as Platonism would gradually come to eliminate any external constraints on production by the ultimate One. To that crucial development we shall now turn.

It is through pagan monotheism that the concept of transcendence came to the fore in late antiquity. Grasping this historical point is of the utmost importance to the story of Augustine and the development of Catholic theology. Western civilization owes to the pagan tradition its philosophical conception of transcendence, that is, the idea of the existence of an intelligible world free from space and time. That is a powerful idea in itself and a profoundly radical one when applied to the notion of God. It is also one that is difficult to capture conceptually, since it is hard not to slip into spatial and temporal discourse whenever discussing that transcendent level of existence. Yet today we assume the idea of transcendence when we speak about God. The modern grammar of 'God' encompasses the idea that God does not exist in time and space.

Two modern examples might be useful to clarify this point. Back at the height of the Cold War in 1961, the Soviet Union launched the first cosmonaut into space, Yuri Gagarin. The First Secretary of the Communist Party, Nikita Khrushchev, subsequently reported that Gagarin had failed to see God in outer space, thus confirming the official atheism of the Soviet state. That announcement occasioned considerable puzzlement, precisely because the common cultural notion of God had ceased to include divine existence within the spatial universe. Or consider the events that transpired in California in 1997 when the comet Hale-Bopp unexpectedly emerged in the solar system and passed close to earth. The members of a small UFO cult, Heaven's Gate, used this opportunity to commit suicide in order for their souls to hitch a ride on the comet. That grim event seems perplexing, yet it would have sense in antiquity, especially to Manichees. For God was largely envisioned in the ancient world in spatial terms and understood to exist in or beyond the higher reaches of the visible heavens. But the Platonic idea of transcendence gradually put an end to this thinking, shifting the plane of divine existence from a distant physical dwelling place to a higher level of reality immediately present but unseen. God would now be understood to be nowhere and yet also present everywhere in a non-spatial sense. Moreover, the spiritual vector to that new reality would no longer be up and out into the sky above, but down into the depths of the inner self. An entirely new way to think about God and the soul was now possible.

It was pagan Platonism that initiated this conception of transcendence. To understand it we need to grasp its wider meaning, including especially this turn into the inner self. But first we need to recognize that for Platonists transcendence was a level of reality to be attained by the soul, and not just a speculative theory. That higher level of perfection was accessible to the soul when it turned its moral attention away from the distractions of the mundane world of time and change. This allowed the soul to concentrate on its highest natural power, the intellect, and through its exercise discover anew the world of true being. In doing so, the soul could come not just to discern intellectually another reality, but it could achieve a deep connection within itself to that higher reality which was its source. In the language of the Platonist tradition, the soul could 'share in' or 'participate in' the world of being, and in the process become more real. So the turn into the inner self was a spiritual advance, a turn away from what was external and alien to what was interior and true. Throughout its history, Platonists called this act of interior restoration 'contemplation'. It was understood to be what the practice of philosophy was ultimately about, and it required that the philosopher practice intellectual, moral and physical discipline in order to achieve it. In doing so, the whole self was directed towards that goal of transcendence, not just the intellect alone. Thus, to break through into eternal being through contemplation was to give the outer world of space and time the slip and to become more real. It was to participate in immortality, eternity and divinity in ways that the soul untrained in philosophy could scarcely imagine. Indeed, it was to achieve, while embodied, some measure of the life of the gods, and it presaged an afterlife free from the need for reincarnation. What is perhaps more striking still is that this promise of transcendence was latent in all humans, even if they were unaware of it because of the occluding force of their earthly passions. But when pursued with the full force of the inner self, philosophy promised transcendence of the human condition.

This was the way that Platonism appeared to early Christians, as a religious philosophy promising access to transcendence. It offered its pagan adherents a path to raise the soul into the presence of the divine and eternal. That is how Justin Martyr, the first Christian philosopher and a younger contemporary of Celsus, described Platonism, based on his own brief adherence it (Justin Martyr, *Dialogue with Trypho* 2.6):

> And the thought of immaterial things seized me, and the contemplation of the forms gave wings to my understanding, so that in a short time I saw myself as having become wise, and as a result of this stupidity I expected immediately to behold God. For that is the goal of Plato's philosophy.

This description is laced with disappointment, for Justin came to distrust the promise of Platonism in the same way that Augustine would several centuries later. Platonism would develop in very important ways during those intervening years, so that the version that Augustine came to know was even more clearly religious in its character. That was due in particular to the teachings of Plotinus, the greatest Platonist of late antiquity and the principle philosophical influence on Augustine. We need now to consider the later innovative Platonism that Augustine read.

Plotinus was an Egyptian who was said to have converted to the life of a philosopher when he was twenty-eight years old in 233. He studied in the Hellenistic cultural capital of Alexandria with a rather mysterious teacher, Ammonius Saccas, who seems to have combined serious philosophical reflection with the practice of a disciplined life. After an aborted attempt to visit India in order to study the teachings of the Brahmins, Plotinus set up his school in Rome where he taught, surrounded by both pagan and Christian students, until his death in 270. In his own philosophical work, Plotinus initiated a detailed and compelling articulation of pagan monotheism (Kenney 1991). Above all, he established the absolute centrality of an ultimate first principle, the One or the Good, from which all levels of reality were exclusively derived. To that end he jettisoned the ancient Platonist commitment to an independent material principle. All things emerged into finite existence from the One alone. This process of 'emanation' or 'procession' was an unconstrained overflowing of the inner life of the One. According to Plotinus, the One did not produce the cosmos out of necessity but as an expression of its own inner goodness and fecundity. Moreover, in his greatest intellectual innovation, Plotinus came to understand the One as infinite, as entirely unbounded by any concept or thought. It was, therefore, beyond human description or speculative appraisal. As such it could not really be known about, but rather the soul could only come into communion with it by a presence that transcends knowledge. That could be effected through the practice of a philosophical life leading to interior contemplation, and only through that path. It is by participation in the transcendent that we can come into the immediate presence of the One, by passing through levels of discourse into the silence of the infinite. That can occur only when the soul is sufficiently free from all passions that keep it earthbound, and even from all attachment to theoretical descriptions of the One.

Because the One is infinite, our finite discourse about it can at best serve to provide the soul with a spiritual vector towards it, to be surrendered as the soul unites with the One. Porphyry, a student of Plotinus who edited his works and wrote his biography, believed that Plotinus achieved that state of transcendent union four times during the decade or so that he knew him. Porphyry only managed that exalted state just once. Such attestations indicate how seriously Platonists regarded this state of enlightenment. It meant that the soul had reversed its emanation from the One and moved beyond the material world back towards ever-deeper levels of reality. This transcendentalism was the central commitment Platonism, locating it as the most resolute opponent of materialism in late antiquity. But it also allowed Platonism to offer a revisionist account of the traditional pantheon, with the gods now understood to be powers that emerged from the divine One alone. Because the One was the infinite source of all reality, it was therefore thought to be omnipresent in all things proportionate to their place in the hierarchy of reality. The gods were each immaterial beings who captured an aspect or characteristic of the One. And again, because the One was infinite, it was regarded not as a personal being, but as the source of what we think of as individual personality, first expressed at the level of the gods and then at the human level. In this regard the One, though ultimate, was described by Plotinus as 'a long life stretched out'; the ontological foundation of all finite reality. It was not a finite being to which we can associate, for its infinity precludes the degree of separation requisite for such a relation. But the magnetism of its infinite perfection was understood to draw the soul towards itself, even if there was no direct intentionality involved, for the infinite One resisted such impoverished, finite description. Yet it was to the transcendent One that all souls seek to return: 'The flight of the alone to the alone.'

# Immaterial Truth

Whoever told Augustine to read Platonism knew what he was doing. Augustine tells us in the *Confessions* that his career had taken him from Carthage first to Rome, and then to Milan, where the imperial court was located. He had advanced to exalted social heights, having become the official rhetorician of the capital, charged with giving speeches before the court and the emperor. He had made it to the pinnacle of his profession and a marriage into the Roman Christian aristocracy had been negotiated. He could also expect some important post in the future in the service of the emperor, and with it considerable wealth. One condition of this advancement was to be baptized as a Catholic, in deference to the senatorial family whose daughter he was marrying, and so he enrolled as a catechumen, without any conviction. He still retained his adolescent view of the intellectual deficiencies of that faith, compounded by his years as a Manichaean critic of it. Although Manichees had helped him in his career, he had by now given that up and slipped into a moderate, Ciceronian scepticism. He had never rejected his belief in a final judgement of the soul after death, but otherwise he was agnostic. In this spiritually ambiguous state, he reports that he went to hear Ambrose, the aristocratic Catholic bishop of Milan and celebrated rhetorician, drawn mainly by professional curiosity. There he was surprised by what he heard. For Ambrose had the ability to articulate the beliefs of his religion rationally and persuasively, and could in particular offer plausible readings of Old Testament passages that had previously offended Augustine. Behind that exegesis was a sophisticated understanding of God that intrigued Augustine. Someone in the Catholic circle around Ambrose suggested that he read Platonism. He obtained 'some books of the Platonists' from a man he says was puffed with pride in his philosophical knowledge, presumably a pagan. The treatises that he read were works of Plotinus and Porphyry, translated from Greek into Latin by Marius Victorinus, a Roman senator and convert to Catholicism. What he read overwhelmed him.

Here are two passages from Augustine's earliest works, written before his baptism, that offer a contemporaneous record of his reaction to the Platonist treatises. The first is from *On the Happy Life* 1.4. He is addressing the dedicatee of the work, his friend Manlius Theodorus:

> After reading a few books of Plotinus, for whom I gather you are very keen, I compared them as best I could with the authority of those who handed down the divine mysteries, and I was so inflamed that I'd have broken away from all anchors, if the judgment of several men hadn't forced me back.

We can see here what he is up to – reading Plotinus with an eye towards the sacred scriptures in order to find a new, spiritual method for reading them. His enthusiasm is so strong that he was ready to change his life entirely until those counselling moderation dissuaded him. The second passage is even more vivid in its breathless excitement. It comes from another contemporaneous source, *Against the Academics*, dedicated to his hometown patron and old friend Romanianus. At 2.2.5, he addresses Romanianus, who had become a Manichee, about the books of the Platonists:

> And notice, when certain rich books exhaled over us, as Celsinus says, costly substances from Arabia, and poured a few tiny drops of the most precious perfume onto that little flame, incredibly, Romanianus, incredibly, and even more powerfully than you might believe about me – what more can I say? – unbelievable even to me, those books excited within me a conflagration. What now was honor to me? Or human pomp? Or lust for empty fame? And, finally, what consolation or bond in this mortal life then moved me? Truly I was returning completely to myself. As if on a journey, I confess, I looked back upon that religion which had been grafted into us as boys and entwined in our marrow. Indeed it was taking hold of me but I didn't realize it. And so, hesitatingly, I grabbed the works of the apostle Paul. For I must admit that surely those apostles could not have lived – as they really did live – if their writings and their reasons were opposed to such a good. I read all of it intently and carefully.

Again, the Platonist works ignited an overwhelming desire to live the philosophical life. But they also incited Augustine to read the Christian scriptures, in this case Paul.

What happened next is arresting, and it determined the subsequent course of Augustine's life. He tells us that he had an experience of the Christian God catalysed by reading pagan Platonism. What he found in the Platonists books was the idea of transcendence along with the associated practice of interior contemplation. But he did not just come to grasp the idea of transcendence intellectually; he says that he experienced an immediate cognition that was indubitable and his soul entered into the presence of divine truth. All doubts dissipated and he emerged with an absolute certainty of the existence of God. Let's have a look at his description of this remarkable event from *Confessions* VII.10.16:

> Thus admonished to return to myself, I entered into my innermost depths with you as my guide, and I was able to do so because you had become my helper. I entered and with the eye of my

soul, such as it was, saw above that eye of the soul an immutable light higher than my mind – not the everyday light visible to all bodies, nor a greater light of the same type that might shine more clearly and fill everything with its magnitude. It was not that light but another, entirely different from all others. Nor was it above my mind in the way that oil is on top of water or the sky is above the earth. Rather it was superior because it made me, and I was inferior because I was made by it.

The passage begins with a recognition of the need to turn away from the material world and its distractions, and instead to focus on interior contemplation. He was clear about the fact that he could to do so only through divine assistance, not by any natural capability of his own. Whatever had happened to him was not the result of a disciplined life as a philosopher, but was unmerited. With inner vision – with the eye of the soul – Augustine says that he discovered a light that was clearly not the visible and material light of Manichaeism. It was instead a light accessible to reason, and it was moreover the intelligible light that had created the self into which it was shining. This extraordinary claim is then developed further, disclosing the divine nature to the soul:

Whoever knows the truth knows it, and whoever knows it knows eternity. Love knows it. O eternal truth and true love and beloved eternity, you are my God. To you I sigh day and night. When I first knew you, you raised me up so that I might see that what I saw was being, and that I who saw it was not yet being. And you repelled the weakness of my gaze by shining ardently upon me and I shuddered with love and awe. And I discovered myself far from you in a region of dissimilarity and heard, as it were, a voice from on high: I am the bread of the fully grown; grow and you will feed on me. And you will not change me into yourself, as with food for your body, but you will be changed into me.

Here we have Augustine's account of this breakthrough to divine transcendence. It occurred within the soul and was not based on the external, material world. Nor was it a psychological experience from which observations might be drawn. It was, instead, an act of knowing by which the reality of God was disclosed. That eternal truth was also divine love, a love that had initiated this interior ascension.

This is what God is for Augustine: eternal truth and love itself, transcendent of this lower world. The passage makes plain that God is true being, using Platonic language to describe this transcendent reality. But the soul is not yet capable of sustaining that association. It shudders in awe and love at the force of divine attention upon it, and, too weak to remain in the divine presence, it falls away to a level of reality consistent with its deficient moral character. Real knowledge of God is achieved, therefore, by the interior presence of God within the soul, and this is possible only with divine aid. The power of divine love active within the soul can alone accomplish this. The eucharistic imagery of the passage underscores this need, to be met by participation in Catholic Christianity.

Augustine then returns to his fundamental problem, his inability to grasp immaterial reality:

And I said: But truth can't just be nothing even if it is not diffused through finite or infinite space? And you cried from far off: 'Truly, I am who am.' And I heard as one hears in the heart, and from that moment there was no longer any doubt. It would have been easier to doubt that I was alive than that there is no truth perceived by the intellect through the things that are made.

That is the voice of God from Exod. 3.14, annunciating his absolute reality.

Augustine has now discerned with utter certainty that there exists a divine level of reality that is non-spatial and eternal. He knows this not just conceptually, but also personally, because by God's power his soul has given space and time the slip. While only instantaneous, this knowledge of transcendent truth is indubitable.

It is worth stopping for a moment to notice how important this idea of God as truth is to Augustine. Indeed, the connection of God with truth is fundamental for Augustine. He says in a subsequent passage – *Confessions* VII.17.23 – that the foundations of his aesthetic judgements had previously perplexed him. Remember he had been in a sceptical frame of mind beforehand. But not so sceptical that he ceased to believe that souls would be judged after death for their actions. That suggests that he had some latent commitment to ethical standards according to which human actions could be assessed. He goes on to explain how his pondering of value judgements led to an immediate insight of God as truth itself. Just as we saw in Augustine's first account at *Confessions* VII.10.16, this passage describes his immediate knowledge of a transcendent God discoverable by interior contemplation. But the passage does more than that, and disquietingly so. It also picks up on the soul's inability to sustain contemplation of God, first intimated in the earlier account. Then the soul fell back from the brightness of the divine light. The second ascension narrative makes that sense of failure much more starkly evident. Here is how the narrative begins:

> And I marveled that at last I loved you, not a phantom in place of you. Yet I was not stable enough to enjoy my God, but was swept up to you by your beauty and then torn away from you by my weight. I collapsed with a groan into inferior things. That weight was my sexual habit. Yet the memory of you remained with me and I had no sort of doubt to whom I should cling, though I was not yet able to do that.

There is much here that requires unpacking. First, the concept of 'weight', a term that Augustine often uses to refer to the focus of desire, to the preponderance of love. Later in the *Confessions* (XIII.9.10) he says: 'My weight is my love. Wherever I am taken, my love takes me there.' In the passage quoted above, the tension is between two sharply conflicted loves: love of the beauty of God and love for earthly things. The term that he uses for this weight is *consuetudo carnalis*, which can broadly refer to a habitual focus on material things, somewhat like the term 'the flesh' in the epistles of St. Paul. That would certainly fit his pursuit of success, wealth and prestige in his career as a rhetorician. But in the *Confessions*, it also carries the more specific sense of a sexual habit. Augustine's carefully crafted spiritual autobiography has prepared the reader for this claim by accentuating his sexual compulsions. We hear about his specifically sexual habits throughout the early books (*Confessions* II.2.2-3; II.3.6-8; III.1.1; III.3.5; IV.2.2). These disclosures culminate in the claim that he satisfied his insatiable sexual desires with intensity, and that this habit held him captive and tortured him (*Confessions* VI.12.21-23). Because of his impending marriage to the daughter of an aristocratic Catholic family, he was forced to send his long-term concubine away. While she returns to North

Africa vowing to live a celibate life, he promptly takes a temporary mistress. Later, in Book Eight, he too will find the strength through divine assistance 'to follow the example of a woman' and make a vow of celibacy. This tale of his sexually dysfunctional state explains why his soul collapses back into the ruts of habit. It is only through the power of God within his soul that he was granted this visionary moment of contemplation in the first place. He portrays himself as entirely unprepared for divine contemplation, conspicuously lacking the discipline of a philosophical life. But these moments of contemplation happened anyway, through an act of divine self-disclosure, and he became certain of the existence of God. Here is Augustine's second description of this moment of contemplation:

Then I was inquiring why I approved the beauty of bodies, whether celestial or terrestrial, and on what basis I made unqualified judgments about mutable things, saying: this ought to be thus and that ought not to be thus. While asking on what basis I made the judgments I was making, I discovered the unchanging and actual eternity of truth above my changeable mind. And so by stages I went from bodies to the soul which senses through the body, and from there to its inner force, to which bodily senses report external things; that is as far as beasts can go. And from there I went on to the power of reasoning to which is referred for judgment that which arises from the bodily senses. This power itself, ascertaining within me its mutability, raised itself up to its own understanding. It led its thinking away from that which is habitual, withdrawing itself from contradictory swarms of fantasies so that it might discover the light strewn upon it, and then, without any doubt, it could declare that the immutable is preferable to the mutable. On this basis it could know the immutable, for unless it could know the immutable in this way, there would be no way to prefer the immutable to the mutable with certainty. And so in the flash of a trembling glance it reached that which is. Then I clearly saw your invisible things understood through the things that are made. But I did not have the strength to keep my gaze fixed. My weakness rebounded and I returned to my customary state. I bore with me only a cherished memory and a desire, as it were, for something I had smelled but could not yet eat.

Here Augustine charts the interior geography of his soul. The focus of his consciousness moves through the layers of his person: first the material and bodily level, then the psychological stages of outward perception and inner sensation, and then rational reflection. As the soul continues its inner journey, the rational element removes its attention from judgements about sensations and shifts to the conceptual foundations for those judgements. Then it comes to grasp the immutable first principles of material existence. Within the created depths of the innermost self, the soul reaches eternal reality. In that instantaneous flash – a moment out of time – the soul discovers the immutable, the eternal, the transcendent.

What was disclosed in these moments of contemplation became the foundation of Augustine's life and thought. However fleeting, they were instances of certainty that changed everything for him. And what was disclosed was transcendent reality, a hitherto unknown level discoverable not in space and time, but free from both, and accessed through the inner self. He realized that during all his years as a Manichee he had been misguided. His thinking had been locked into a materialistic account of reality, confined to the physical universe, and centred on a primitive theory of cosmic warfare. But now an entirely new understanding of the nature of things had flooded his consciousness, overwhelming the categories of his former way of imagining the divine. For what had occurred, he insists, was no mere act of the imagination, no purely theoretical grasp of some novel philosophical idea. He had been utterly changed in his reflections by a deep knowledge that had come upon the innermost recesses of his soul. Unbidden, this moment of sudden enlightenment brought before his intellect an immediate grasp of what is real and eternal. And it simultaneously disclosed the utter poverty of his spiritual state. To know the transcendent in this immediate fashion involved more than just the conceptual capacity of the intellect, but implicated the moral nature of the soul as well. To know the perfect and the eternal required moral purification and stability. But Augustine's soul was anything but pure and stable. So this extraordinary knowledge of the divine was an entirely unmerited gift to him by God, an act of divine disclosure that at once gave him certainty of the reality of God and of the moral poverty of his soul.

Both aspects of this disclosure warrant further reflection. Let's first consider the shape of reality as Augustine now understood it.

His cognition of transcendence alerted him to the fact that reality is not as it appears to ordinary consciousness. That everyday perspective captures, as it were, a too narrow spectrum. To say this is not merely to suggest that the range of phenomena exceeds our capacity for physical appraisal, as for example in the case of subatomic particles. Augustine is saying something far more radical. He now regards material reality, however it is discerned, to be just one level of being. He has come to discover that there are degrees of reality, so that 'being' can be understood to have levels. From that recognition several vitally important insights emerged. First, there are different sorts of things that exist, and they can be graded in terms of the quality of their being. Thus, plants can be described as less real than mammals, while humans are more real than either. Each type of thing manifests a different level of consciousness and has different levels of agency. This is the so-called 'great chain of being', derived from Platonism, which became a staple of medieval metaphysics.

But more important for Augustine's theology is the recognition that, while humans have a natural place on the chain of being, they are also unique in their ability to change the value of their being. Humans can become more or less real, depending on their moral focus, and on the extent to which they concentrate upon their divine source. By engaging in interior contemplation, they can begin to participate more deeply in divine transcendence, in eternal being itself. Augustine believed that he had been shown exactly this through interior ascension. This means that the human soul has a 'cursive' quality, to use computer jargon. It can, as it were, click on different levels of being and value. It can choose more or less goodness, more or less love and thus more or less reality. Our souls have spiritual mobility. The interior disclosure of transcendence alerted Augustine to previously undiscovered modes of reality and to the possibility that his soul could become more real, more stable and perhaps even eternal. Thus, for Augustine, this breakthrough to the transcendent shifted the consciousness of his soul towards a different sense of its own spiritual location. It opened up a map, charting his soul's current location over against a range of spiritual possibilities. Yet that was painful, as his soul's plunge down from the transcendent to the material level made evident. But it also offered the possibility for advancing beyond his present zone of reality. How that might be achieved will become his next major issue, something that we will explore further as we track the unfolding of Augustine's thought.

There remains the question of how this moment of transcendence helped him address the nature and origin of evil, something that he had said plagued him both in his Manichaean period and immediately thereafter. As we saw, he believed that his commitment to materialism stood in the way of a resolution to evil and its existence. So how did transcendence allow him to peer down into the deep well of evil and come to terms with what he saw? The answer is complex and requires unravelling. Its keys are the ideas we have just considered: the notion of degrees of reality and the cursive nature of the soul.

First, we need to begin by exploring the significance of gradations of being in reference of evil. In his rejection of Manichaeism, Augustine jettisoned dualism. He regards transcendence as the core insight that cleared the way for his acceptance of Christian monotheism precisely because it showed him with certainty that there is only one true reality. Only God, the Good, is really real. There is nothing else that has true being, because the One God is infinite. There is no opposite power on the same plane of reality with the infinite One. And the reality of God is absolute and ultimate. Everything else is dependent upon it, either directly or indirectly. Those finite things that have come into existence have only relative existence. They neither absolutely exist – like God – nor do they entirely lack being. They exist because they come from God, but they are not wholly real, since they are not God. That then opens up a new grasp of evil. He says that whatever things exist are good, and evil into whose origins he had been inquiring is not a substance, for if it were a substance, it would be good (*Confessions* VII.12.18). And so evil has no being, that is, it is not a fixed substance. It is, instead, an epiphenomenon of divine creation. Evil is the vector of away from God, and has no independent claim to reality. Augustine insists that these are insights that emerged from those transformative moments of contemplation. He saw these truths intellectually and they were made clear to him immediately. He does not infer them from the experience. Instead he discerned these truths immediately, clearly and indubitably. So Augustine's account of the non-being of evil is not just a metaphysical theory, but something that he regards as ineluctably disclosed in a moment of interior contemplation. We will return to explore the larger implications of this understanding of evil in Chapter 4.

With this representation of evil as the privation of goodness and being comes the recognition of its irrational origins in the will. That understanding too is knit into his contemplative recognition of levels of reality. Augustine maintains that his inquiry into the nature of evil led him to discover its source in the perversity of the human will. Human volition twisted the soul away from the highest reality of the Good. In so doing, it abandoned its innermost self and swelled with what is external to it. Note that this is an act of perverse self-abandonment for Augustine, a loss of the intimate for the external. By fleeing from the highest being of God, the soul slips away from its own highest reality as well, preferring instead what is inferior to itself. The soul is restricted in its ability to associate with God because of its own self-constructed moral identity. It seeks a false individuation, a diminished existence fraught with contingency. Thus, we see stitched together here the two main themes of Augustine's account of evil, non-being and irrationality, both direct insights from contemplation.

To know God as transcendent is, for Augustine, to know that the soul is not capable of sustaining the presence of God. Moreover, the soul is what it now is by its own choice. This fact is something that we suppress from ourselves, a wisdom too terrible to bear, a self-knowledge to be assiduously avoided. That is why Augustine regards the root of evil to be pride, the soul's choice of a false self, a disordered self-will that desires to separate from God in the interest of creative self-regard. What is particularly insidious is the effect this has on our ability to know God. Our place in reality is conditioned by the degree of separation from God that we have chosen. Several essential points follow from this. First, the soul may come to regard reality as only what it is accustomed to seeing in its present state. Indeed, the soul may come to insist on this and reject higher modes of knowing. For Augustine, this is the moral foundation of materialism, an insistence that only what is physical is real. The fallen state of the soul conditions it to desire this to be true, and to resist any account of a deeper level of reality. In his earlier, disordered moral state as a Manichee, Augustine was – in his judgement – an example of this phenomenon. So for Augustine, materialism is not just a failed, diminished account of reality, it is also a doubling down on the moral self-impoverishment of the fallen soul. Rejection of divine transcendence is grounded, therefore, in a refusal to accept the self-disclosure required for the soul to overcome its false identity and return to the presence of infinite being. Indeed, Augustine seems to have drafted his autobiography in part to expose the truth about himself to himself, and to offer a demonstration of how that can be accomplished to others.

Augustine was well aware of the pervasiveness of that human refusal to accept transcendence and its moral roots in a perverse resistance to interior self-reflection. Late in the *Confessions*, he is insistent that he had indeed had immediate knowledge of divine transcendence within his soul. He is indignant at Christian opponents who rejected that claim (*Confessions* XII.11.11-12). Using auditory language that picks up on the divine voice from *Confession* VII.10.16, he repeats over and over the attestation of this revelation: 'You spoke to me, Lord, with a strong voice in my inner ear ... .' His claim of divine transcendence rested on his experience of interior contemplation and he would not allow that personal revelation to be impeached. He had certain knowledge of God's transcendence; this was the revelatory basis for his turn from materialism to Catholic Christianity. Yet if we reflect on his trajectory, we can also discern that his conversion was not just a rejection of Manichaean materialism and dualism. It was also an implicit rejection of the North African Catholicism of his childhood. For that too was inadequate in this regard, lacking as it did a way to describe God in ways that were not anthropomorphic. He admits that in his youth he could not think of God except in earthly and human terms. That was the sort of orthodox theology that the Manichees ridiculed. So, to accept the sophisticated transcendentalism preached by Ambrose was to convert to a form of Catholicism previously unknown to him. Only then could his soul know the one true God, the transcendent and eternal creator. But to sustain that insight he needed to take up the discipline of Catholicism, now understood in a deeper and more authentic fashion. To that new theology we shall now turn.

# 2

# God

*Eternal truth and true love and beloved eternity,*
*you are my God.*

To believe in one God is to believe in more than can be said. As Augustine once told his North African congregation (Sermon 52, vi, 16): 'If you comprehend God, that is not God.' Some months after the contemplative experiences that so transformed him, Augustine wrote that God is 'better known by ignorance' than by description (*On Order* 2.16.44). If one could get beyond fragmentary images of God and concentrate on the truth behind them, 'then one can investigate divine matters – not just as things to be believed, but rather as things to be truly contemplated, grasped, and held onto'. God is, therefore, best known by a learned ignorance, *docta ignorantia*, to use his phrase from a later letter (*Letter* 130.28). That would remain his position throughout his long life, a conviction grounded in his immediate experience of transcendence.

Augustine was not alone in such thinking; indeed, he was part of a growing movement across the ancient world that gradually revolutionized the meaning of God. Emphasis on the unknowability of God signalled a commitment to divine transcendence. If God really transcends the world of space and time, then God must be beyond the range of finite reflection, barely on the horizon of the intellect. While no description of God can, therefore, really stick, yet a grammar of 'God' was nonetheless needed to direct the soul towards the divine and – in a certain sense – to locate God properly beyond finitude. Conceptual scaffolding was erected in late antiquity, across several theological traditions, to frame this new understanding of God, even if no descriptive claim could be adequate.

So 'God' has a past, for the emergence of Western monotheism was a lengthy and multidimensional process. The God of Christianity developed through the centuries, layered by accretion as new ideas were added to its semantic field. Some of the most important elements, including the concept of transcendence itself, had roots in pagan philosophy – as we have just seen. Some philosophical ideas were superimposed over earlier scriptural ones; others migrated and were traded across traditions, so that discourse about God became a set of conceptual variations on a cluster of common themes. As we might expect, such a significant change in the theological representation of God was associated with alterations in religious practice. Scholars have recently come to recognize powerful changes in the religions of late antiquity, especially a widespread shift away from blood sacrifice to different modes of religious activity, including asceticism, monasticism and scriptural exegesis (Strousma 2008, 2016). The obsolescence of blood sacrifice cut across the spectrum of religious traditions, affecting them in different ways. Both rabbinic Judaism and Christianity are the products of the violent collapse of the sacrificial monotheism of ancient Israel following the Roman destruction of the Jerusalem temple in AD 70. Each is a 'post-sacrificial' successor of ancient Israelite religion. Meanwhile, the pagan tradition retained its sacrificial tradition, though the meaning of sacrifice was gradually revised through the efforts of philosophical interpreters, especially the Platonists.

The widespread move away from sacrifice was undoubtedly important in its own right. But of greater historical importance was the underlying shift in what might be called the 'spiritual location' of the divine. The decline of sacrifice was historically coincident with the emergence of the conception of divine transcendence, the idea of a God who did not dwell in the physical heavens and savour the sweet odour of burnt offerings rising up through the clouds. A God beyond the physical cosmos was a God beyond space and time. And it was a God who was omnipresent precisely because he was not on the spatial grid. Such a God was everywhere and nowhere, no longer above and beyond, but deep down and within. For that was the true religious vector now: into the spiritual self where another dimension of reality could be accessed.

It was that compelling recognition that brought Augustine to Catholic Christianity through the catalysis of Platonism.

The texts we have just considered in Chapter 1 demonstrate the transformative force that the experience of divine transcendence had on him. Now we need to consider the larger understanding of God that Augustine articulated as he began to practice Catholic Christianity. To get at that, we will need to examine the ultimate experience of God described in the *Confessions*, the vision at Ostia. That followed Augustine's baptism at Easter in 387 and defined his understanding of God for the remainder of his life. The sections of the *Confessions* that follow that account are, in many respects, an effort to unpack this culminating ascension into God. From it emerged Augustine's mature conception of God and the soul. This chapter will trace out the lineaments of that understanding, looking carefully at Augustine's distinctive account of the God of classical Christianity.

# Soliloquies

You cannot be a spectator of the infinite. That is something the experience of contemplation impressed upon Augustine. From the immediacy of contemplation, Augustine realized that God is not just unknowable because he is infinite, not just too vast to capture with the finite tools of the mind. While that is true, there is much more involved. For, if God is infinite, he must be omnipresent to finite reality, permeating finite things and sustaining their existence. God is, therefore, not just incommensurable with finite beings, but also totally present to them. As the continuous source of existence for every finite thing at every moment, God is not something that you could know about – precisely because there is no neutral zone from which to observe God. The omnipresence of God thus precludes knowing God after the fashion of our knowledge of things in the world. That radical recognition about God is something that underlies much of Augustine's writing. It helps to explain his overpowering sense of the immediacy of God, a God who knew Augustine's inner nature better than he did himself. This insight helps to clarify as well the painful sense of intimate loss that pervades his thought, the longing for a return to a more consummated state of union with this omnipresent divine source.

It was in 'the books of the Platonists' that Augustine first discovered the conception of a transcendent God, the infinite and omnipresent source of finite reality. As we saw in Chapter 1, he tells us in the seventh book of the *Confessions* that its truth was then confirmed by contemplative union with God. That Christian enlightenment led him to recognize God as 'eternal truth and true love and beloved eternity'. This knowledge was so complete that he could more easily doubt his own existence than doubt the reality of God. That is because this contemplative knowledge was not spectator knowledge about God, but something else entirely. It is crucial for us, as contemporary readers of Augustine, to capture this point. Our default position is to assume that real knowledge is based on independent observation, in which a knower suppresses any personal perspective in order to grasp what is known 'objectively'. That tacit model of knowledge has permeated Western discourse about God since the late medieval period. But it is not how Augustine, or his Platonist sources, understood contemplative knowledge of God.

To clarify this claim, we need to reflect briefly on two aspects of Platonic transcendentalism. First, is what has been called the 'philosophical economy' of Platonism (Cherniss 1965). Ancient Platonism offered a single account for the foundations of ethics, epistemology and ontology. That account was based on the famous Platonic theory of forms, of immaterial and unchanging paradigms upon which the sensible things in our changing world are dependent. The postulation of transcendent forms or ideas offered the possibility of a unified account that explained the standards employed in value judgement, the basis of true knowledge, and the stability found within the flux of sensible experience. To serve as a unified account, the theory of ideas requires a commitment to degrees of reality, such that the transcendent ideas are more real than the phenomena whose existence they underwrite. Critical is the additional claim that the constituents of the lower world of becoming have a share in the forms; that they participate in their being. So the ideas are more real than their ontological products, and are causes of their diminished reality. That is, of course, the basis for the theory's protreptical force, since it invites us to achieve a higher level of reality, to participate more deeply in what is eternal and completely real. Contemplation is, therefore, the fruition of the soul's desire to reassert its connection more completely to that higher, transcendent world. Its roots are there and in contemplation it can come into a direct relation with the divine, leaving behind – even if only momentarily – its fractured, confused and embodied existence. But this moment out of time ends, returning the soul to its ordinary state of diminished being and its embodied consciousness. That is what Augustine says happened to him. He had unmediated knowledge of the transcendent ideas in the divine Wisdom, the creative intellect of God. In doing so he did not stand apart from Wisdom and discern the archetypes of creation within it. Rather, he had an immediate communion with Wisdom itself, 'touching it' with the full force of love.

To understand this striking depiction of knowledge of the divine, we need to probe a second aspect of Platonism, one to which we have just alluded. It follows directly from the philosophical economy of Platonism: the correlation of levels of knowledge with the soul's participation in being. Platonists regarded the conceptual reasoning that we ordinarily employ as only the threshold level of knowledge. This type of reasoning is inherently intentional, such that the objects of theoretical appraisal are distinct from the knowing subject. But higher-level knowledge of transcendent reality, what the Platonists called 'understanding', is possible only if the subject has been purified of the passions that occlude the soul in its exercise of intellection and lead to illusions driven by desire. The capacity to acquire that knowledge of transcendent reality is, therefore, directly related to the moral character of the knower. Moreover, at the higher reaches of knowledge, the soul can participate in the nature of the ideas – especially their ontological stability, their eternity, their perfection. So for the Platonist tradition, in acquiring true knowledge, the soul leaves behind spectator knowledge and moves towards participatory association between the soul and those transcendent ideas. At its apex is contemplation itself, when the soul achieves unmediated association with the divine. Hence, the Platonist approach was different from our common ways of thinking about knowing. Our default notion assumes that knowledge is aimed at making a true, explanatory representation of the actual world. But Platonism aims at participation of knower with the known. It assumes, moreover, that the soul is, as it were, within the frame of knowledge, since the moral status of the soul directly conditions what it can know. The knower is thus never a neutral spectator, but a participant in the act of knowing and a determinant of what can be known. So for ancient Platonists, a spectator approach to knowledge is inadequate, prone to illusory, passion-driven manipulation of putative truth. Truth yields only to the soul that comes to participate in the transcendent ideas. Another way to put this is that Platonism regards truth not as theoretical and distanced, but as active and associative. But that is challenging to our default thinking, precisely because the moral status of the soul is determinative of what can be known about God.

The upshot of this approach to knowledge for reading Augustine is evident. The deeply embedded practice of regarding knowledge as exclusively a matter of observation and verification is inadequate for understanding his account of the soul's knowledge of God. Any reading of Augustine that is grounded in a spectator model of knowledge, where subject and object are distinct, misses the core of his approach to God. For Augustine the soul's cognition of divine transcendence fails to fit this model, since divine existence is disclosed through interior access of the soul to God. Contemplation is understood as the closure of the soul with God, and thereafter a growing participation of the soul's finite reality in the infinite being of its divine source. There is nothing here to reassure the proponent of spectator knowledge, nested as that model is in the natural phenomena of the material world. The soul's cognition of God cannot, therefore, be captured by what we think of as sensory perception. To know God is to find God within the soul, deep down in the aquifer of our being, at the point where we are sustained by our divine source. This is not to say that the discourse of spectator knowledge does not have a place, only that Augustine recognizes that such discourse is a concession to our earthly existence in time and space. With these observations in mind, we might now turn to Augustine's new theology and his depiction of God in the aftermath of his sudden discovery of divine transcendence.

The place to begin is a treatise that Augustine wrote some months after the enlightenment experience that we considered in Chapter 1. The work is called *Soliloquies* – a word he invented – and it contains a series of interior dialogues between the inner voice of reason and that of Augustine himself. This work allows us to observe Augustine's first theological exposition of how he had come to think about God. It was written in the late autumn of 386 or the winter months of 387, before his baptism. *Soliloquies* is, therefore, a contemporaneous treatise written in the midst of his conversion, a theological self-portrait sketched out about a decade before he wrote the more polished narrative of the *Confessions*. We can, as a result, catch a sense of the freshness of his recent, interior encounter with the transcendent God. We can also observe his initial efforts to articulate what he had discovered in Christian theological language.

*Soliloquies* offers an initial, lengthy prayer that introduces for the first time the unique voice that Augustine later employs throughout the *Confessions*, a work which is throughout addressed to God as a prayer. Here, the reader is invited into the intimacy of the author's presence to God. This unusual dimension allows Augustine to preserve some sense of the immediacy of those earlier moments of transcendence. But Augustine writes within the firmament of time and space, looking back now with a memory of that deeper communion with divine Wisdom. He writes as well in painful remembrance that his communion with God was instantaneous and unsustained because of the moral condition of his soul. Now he seeks the means to heal his soul and to recover that moment of transcendent communion. The first section of the prayer draws on the conversionary insights that had then emerged (*Soliloquies* 1.2):

> God, maker of the universe, first grant that I might rightly beseech you, then that I might act as one worthy to be heard by you, lastly that you might free me. God through whom all things, which would not exist by themselves, strive to exist. You are God who does not permit to perish even that which is prone by itself to destruction. God, who created the world from nothing, which the eyes of all judge to be most beautiful, God, who does not make evil, and makes that which is evil to be not the worst that is possible. God, who reveals to the few, who take refuge in that which truly exists, that evil is nothing. God, because of whom the universe, even with its perverse side, is perfect. God because of whom even extreme dissonance is nothing, since the lesser harmonizes with the better. God whom everything loves that is able to love, whether knowingly or unknowingly. God in whom are all things, yet who is neither defiled by the defilement of all creatures not harmed by their wickedness, nor deceived by their error. God, who has wanted only the pure to know truth. God, father of truth, father of wisdom, father of true and supreme life, father of bliss, father of goodness and beauty, father of intelligible light, father of our awakening and illumination, father of the pledge by which we are admonished to return to you.

The great prayers of Augustine are torrents not of unrequited love, but of remembered intimacy, together with pleas for the gift of its renewal. Here he begins with a call for freedom from the sins that ended his communion with the divine. Then the prayer recognizes God's role as the source of all finite reality, which would not otherwise exist; the sustainer of all things, which would otherwise be destroyed; and the sole creator from nothing of all things that do exist. Augustine then forcefully states that those few who – like himself – have taken refuge in what is really real come to realize that evil is the privation of reality, not a thing in itself. Contemplation of the good itself leads to a recognition that divine perfection underlies the apparent dissonances of the finite world, conducing them into patterns that conform to the divine order. Moreover, all things love and desire God even if only unconsciously. God, who is truly real, remains perfect, even if imperfect things exist in and through him. Crucially, only those whose souls are pure can know God, the father of perfections, who awakens souls and returns them to himself. Each of these theological insights is the fruit of contemplation.

The prayer goes on to explore the nature of a transcendent, divine level of reality (*Soliloquies* 1.3): 'God, whose realm is an entire world unknown to sense perception; God, from whose realm law is transcribed onto this world.' Here we have both the sharp separation of the intelligible level and the sense world, along with the fundamental connection of the former to the latter as the foundation of rational patterns of order. The prayer then powerfully reiterates the same formula, rooted once again in a transcendent level of reality, to underscore the foundation of all things in God (*Soliloquies* 1.3):

I call to you, God, truth, in whom and by whom and through whom all true things are true. God, wisdom, in whom and by whom and through whom all who are wise are wise. God, true and complete life, in whom and by whom and through whom all things live that truly and completely live. God, happiness, in whom and by whom and through whom all things that are happy, are happy. God, the good and the beautiful, in whom and by whom and through whom all things that are good and beautiful are good and beautiful. God, intelligible light, in whom and by whom and through whom all things that shine intelligibly, shine forth intelligibly.

Each of these transcendental ideas – truth, goodness, wisdom, life and so on – gives rise to dependent realities at the lower level of earthly existence. Augustine thought of these transcendent ideas as paradigms within the divine Word, through whom all things were made. Each is a perfect instance and source for the properties that then emerge in the created world. So there may be two levels of reality, but the lower world in space and time is not autonomous, but dependent for its nature and existence on the transcendent realm. It is the unseen that is really real, while what is apparent is only fractionally real.

That profound insight, that startling inversion of ordinary consciousness, carries with it a directive to the soul for moral recalibration. That is something the soul is too weak to accomplish by itself, yet it knows that its true home lies there in the transcendent, the divine, the real. The prayer continues along those lines (*Soliloquies* 1.3):

> God, through whom we learn that what we thought ours is in fact alien to us, and what we thought alien is actually ours. God, through whom we do not cling to the charms and lures of evil things. God, through whom trifles do not diminish us. God, through whom what is superior in us is not subjugated by what is inferior. God, through whom death is swallowed up in victory. God, who converts us. God, who strips us of what is not and clothes us with what is.

That is certainly a striking image: the divine Father clothing the spiritually prodigal soul with a cloak of reality, dispelling its illusions. But, for Augustine, reading the parable of prodigal son is not just an ethical tale of forgiveness, it is a metaphysical lesson about divine being calling souls from the inferior existence into which they are fallen, back to the higher reality that is their true patrimony. This spiritual reading is driven by Augustine's now dispositive recognition of transcendent existence. Because God is absolute reality, God is, paradoxically, both the omnipresent source of all things and also beyond all finite beings: 'God, above whom, and outside whom, and without whom, nothing exists; God, under whom everything exists, in whom everything exists, with whom everything exists' (*Soliloquies* 1.4).

All these claims are not so much descriptions of God as attempts to locate the notion of God at the edge of discourse. Neither are they speculative judgements. When Augustine speaks about God in *Soliloquies,* we can see him struggling to express the consciousness of transcendence that had so recently preceded his writing this work. Then, in a moment of stillness, he believed his soul united with the absolute reality of God. Now, he begs for divine aid to return to that condition (*Soliloquies* 1.4):

> Whatever has been said by me, you are the one God; come to my aid; you, the one, eternal, true substance, where there is no strife, no confusion, no change, no need, no death. Where there is perfect harmony, total clarity, complete stability, supreme plenitude, perfect life. Where nothing is lacking and there is no excess.

It is only because God has been disclosed to him as perfect reality that God can be relied upon, for there is nothing unstable or changing about him. In that moment of transcendence Augustine grasped God's absolute being from out of the misery of his present life. Now he relates how the transcendent exceeds the mundane: no strife, confusion, change, need or death. These are negative descriptors, based on the perfection and plenitude of God's reality as he encountered it.

This contrast between the excellence of transcendence and the relative deficiency of earthly life is the source of what is perhaps the dominant theme in Augustine's spiritual writing: the longing of the soul for God. That longing is existential; it is the magnetism of absolute reality drawing what is merely contingently real towards itself. It is perfection exercising its inherent attraction to the flawed, the good acting as a lure to what has turned away towards evil. These images – of ontological descent from God, of self-imposed exile at lower levels of reality, of prodigal flight down into a debased condition – became the sounding board of Augustine's theology. And, along with these themes, is the image of God as the salvific reality that calls fallen souls out of the darkness of earthly existence into his marvellous divine light, the true homeland of the soul. As Augustine prays in *Soliloquies* 1.5:

> Accept me, your servant, as I flee from these things, just as they accepted me as a foreigner when I fled from you. I realize that

I must come back to you; open up to my knocking; show me how to reach you. I have nothing but my desire; I know nothing except that the fleeting and perishable should be spurned; and the certain and eternal should be sought. This I do, father, since it is all I know; but I am ignorant of how to reach you. Prompt me, show me, and give me provision for the journey. If those who find refuge in you find you through faith, then give me faith; if through virtue, then give me virtue; if through knowledge, then give me knowledge. Increase in me faith, hope and love. O, how marvelous and unique is your goodness.

Whatever it will take to make that return, that is what he desires from God. Here he pleads for whatever would supply the strength to make his return. The prayer concludes with a final plea for interior conversion and a return to the eternal homeland (*Soliloquies* 1.6):

I pray only for your most excellent mercy, so that you may convert me inwardly to you, and allow nothing to prevent me from striving towards you. While I move and carry this my body, command me to be pure, magnanimous, just, prudent, a perfect lover and student of your wisdom, and worthy of a home – a home in your most blessed realm.

These are powerful texts, some of the earliest we have from Augustine. They are filled with an intense memory of divine presence and with a longing for its recovery. They explore the logic of transcendence, the perfection of a realm out of time, the beauty and goodness of God. One can also see entwined the motivating ideas behind his shift to monotheism: a God so real that all other things depend upon it for their existence, and, in consequence, a God who is omnipresent, at the root of whatever has emerged into finite being. But for Augustine, these conceptions were presented in *Soliloquies* as the result of his soul's interior access to God. They are not speculation or theory, but the framing in theological language of a deeper understanding that had overwhelmed him. And they are not the last such effort, only the first, to be succeeded by his account of post-baptismal contemplation in *Confessions* IX. That episode offers us Augustine's definitive treatment of the soul's closure with God. It warrants now our scrutiny.

# Eternal Wisdom

Those texts from *Soliloquies* just considered were written before the event that Augustine describes in *Confessions* IX – the 'vision at Ostia' – in which he and his mother Monica together achieve contemplative knowledge of God. That passage is the pre-eminent description of unmediated knowledge of God in the works of Augustine (*Confessions* IX.10.23-25). But, in contrast, the passages we considered from the *Soliloquies* reflect his earlier conversionary period and his first efforts at Christian theology. They are based on his initial experience of Christian enlightenment, when he was still – on his own account – a confused and sinful soul. Indeed, they were written when he was a Christian by conviction but not in fact, for he was not yet baptized. But the narrative of contemplation in *Confessions* IX is different. Now Augustine is now formally Christian, and, from his perspective, his soul has been transformed by the sacramental power of the baptism.

The culminating visionary narrative of the *Confessions* begins as Augustine and his mother are leaning out a window into an interior garden in the port of Ostia as they await passage back to North Africa. Augustine has given up his worldly career and become not only a Catholic, but also an ascetic. He is determined to return home to North Africa and to live there with his son and some associates in a rural monastery, after having given away his patrimony. Monica's death is imminent but unsuspected, and their conversation turns to the heavenly life of the saints. Augustine then describes how their dialogue leads into a joint interior ascension of their souls to the divine Wisdom. This was a simultaneous episode of transcendence, a momentary apprehension of the heavenly realm into which the soul of Monica would soon enter after her death. The fact that it is a joint experience is notable, as are the differences between the Monica and her son. She, an uneducated woman, achieves the same unmediated knowledge of divine Wisdom as does her son (Kenney, 2005, 2013). That two people are involved also suggests an incipient sense of Christian community and resonates off texts such as Mt. 18.20: 'For where two or three are gathered together in my name, there am I in the midst of them.' Indeed, Augustine makes it clear that they are alone and tranquil together 'in the presence of truth' which is God himself. They strain to grasp conceptually what the eternal and transcendent life of the saint might be like.

What follows are two descriptions of their interior ascent. Here is the first version (*Confessions* IX.10.24):

> And the conversation led us to the conclusion that any pleasure of the bodily senses, in any physical light, was seen as incomparable with the delight of that other life and not worthy of consideration. Raising ourselves up by ardent affection to the self-same, we traversed by stages all corporal things and the earth itself, where the sun and moon and stars shine upon the earth. And we ascended further by interior reflection and dialogue and wonder at your works, and we entered into our minds, and then went beyond them so that we might touch that region of unending abundance where you eternally feed Israel with the food of truth. And there life is the wisdom by which all things are made, both things that and those that will be. But this wisdom is not made, but is as it was and always will be. It is not possible for it to have been in the past or to be in the future, for it just is, since it is eternal. And while we talked and longed for it, we touched it slightly with the full force of the heart. And we sighed and left behind the first fruits of the spirit bound there, as we returned to the sound of our speech where a word has both a beginning and an ending. But what is like your word, our lord, who abides in himself without growing old and renews all things?

We have seen this before, in the interior ascension narratives of *Confessions* VII. Here we again find a description of the cognition of divine wisdom, now a joint one, in which both souls ascend from external conversation into interior reflection and then into higher levels of reality. And once again the contemplative soul passes beyond time and into eternity before descending back into temporal conversation. Here too the presence of divine Wisdom is immediately contacted by each soul. Notice that this is not an account of a sense experience, from which certain judgements might be inferred. It is something else – a description of an act of self-transcendence in which ordinary levels of discourse give way to a higher cognition. It is utterly unlike corporeal experience, even cognitive experience; rather it is the transmutation of personal experience, as the each contemplative's attention ascends through the levels of the soul and beyond itself into association with eternal wisdom. The soul's longing for the divine is requited in an instant by its 'touching' wisdom slightly, only to slip away again into time and conceptual discourse. It is quite striking and puzzling that their souls leave something behind there in eternal wisdom. The Pauline image of 'the first fruits of the spirit' (Rom. 8.23) suggests that each soul has touched the place in the transcendent realm to which it might hope to return after death. It is a premonitory act of transcendence, disclosing to the ascending soul its place in the divine wisdom, its proper station in the divine plan of creation. Each soul discovers where it truly belongs, and where it might return. Yet both the interior ascent and any recovery of this momentary hold on eternity are possible only by divine assistance. Nothing discerned 'in the presence of truth' suggested that the fallen soul has the power of transcendence within its grasp.

The second description of this moment is a masterpiece of Augustine's rhetoric. It is a text whose prose drives forward with great energy and insistence, sharply articulating the incommensurability of the mundane and the transcendent. And it shifts the imagery to audition, capturing the biblical sense of the divine voice, heard here not physically but within the innermost soul (*Confessions* IX.10.25):

> Therefore we said: If to anyone the tumult of the flesh became silent, if the images of earth and water and air became silent, if the heavens became silent, and the very soul became silent to itself and surpassed itself by not thinking of itself, if all dreams and visions in the imagination became silent, and all speech and every sign and whatever is transitory became silent – for if anyone could hear them, they would all say: 'We did not make ourselves, but he made us who abides in eternity' – if, having said this and directed our ears to him who made them, they were to be silent, then he alone would speak not through them but through himself. We would hear his word not through the tongue of the flesh, nor through the voice of an angel, nor through the sound of thunder, nor through the obscurity of a likeness. Instead we would hear him, whom we love in these things, alone and without them. It was thus when we extended ourselves and in a flash of thought touched the eternal wisdom that abides beyond all things. If this could continue, and all other visions of a much lesser sort could be withdrawn, then this alone would ravish and absorb and enfold the beholder in inward joy. Eternal life is of the quality of

that moment of understanding for which we sighed. Is this not the meaning of 'enter into the joy of your lord'? And when will that be? When we all rise again but are not all changed.

This text makes plain what true knowledge of God is in this life. It is an anticipation of the final state of the soul, when its fallen nature will be transformed and come into the immediate presence of God. Note that this is a moment of understanding – now a moment in time, but then a moment in the transcendent present of eternity. What grounds this passage is the central insight of Augustine's conversion, that there is a higher, divine level of reality beyond time and space. Here we see that all the joys and pleasures of our present life have their source there, and while they betoken that other realm, they also subtly occlude it. So too does the finite imagery of language play a mixed role; it offers only the obscurity of likeness, the limited disclosure of any distanced appraisal. For Augustine, therefore, real knowledge of God cannot be conceptual and it cannot be descriptive. Neither is it theoretical. Here at Ostia it is unmediated, unitive, deeply participatory. It is also unsustainable for the embodied soul still living its journey in time. Any symbolic and conceptual discourse about the divine must henceforth be seen against this moment of understanding, efficacious to the extent that it directs the soul towards God. It is the language of God's self-disclosure through revelation – attuned to the fallen state of the soul – that will be our best guide.

This description of joint contemplation has a different narrative role than the accounts of earlier interior ascension in book VII. There the issue was discovering transcendence itself. Here, in book IX, the mutual ascent to divine wisdom is framed by the story of Monica's life and death, which occurs shortly thereafter. The story of the vision, or audition, at Ostia both affirms transcendence and intimates what the life of the saints is like. By uniting with the eternal wisdom that abides beyond all things, both souls experience momentarily the joy that ravishes and absorbs and enfolds the saints in eternal union with God. That brief moment of understanding had some of the character of the communion of the saints with divine wisdom. The metaphysical insight that Monica and Augustine achieve is, therefore, explicitly eschatological. It betokens her soul's imminent, post-mortem existence; it marks off the transcendent home where her son might one day join her; and it offers the reader a Christian representation of the soul's transcendent state. Indeed, the passage concludes with a reference to the eschaton, the second coming of Christ and the consummation of time.

Later, in *Confessions* XII, Augustine meditates on this state of transcendence, drawing upon both the pre-baptismal and the Ostian narratives. In order to interpret them retrospectively, he turns to scripture for guidance. This had become his characteristic mode of reflection over the decade since his baptism and subsequent ordination as a priest and bishop. Scripture offered an authoritative basis by which he could articulate and explore the meaning of those remembered moments of contemplation. Pressed by Catholic opponents of his transcendentalism, Augustine insists in starkly personal terms that he has heard in his soul's inner recesses the voice of God. That is the source of his theology. Expanding on the Ostian account, he attests that the divine voice revealed both the transcendence and eternity of God, as well as the first created level of reality, the transcendent heaven – distinct from the physical heaven. What is particularly striking is the fact that Augustine repeatedly grounds the authority for his representation of God in the divine audition to him in contemplation. Here is his account of the nature of God as revealed to him (*Confessions* XII.11.11):

> You have already spoken to me, Lord, with a strong voice in my inner ear, that you are eternal, for you alone have immortality, since you are not changed by any shape or motion, nor is your will altered over time – because no immortal will is one thing and then another. In your sight this is clear to me; may it be more and more clear, I pray you, and in this manifestation may I abide with surety beneath your wings.

This is an exposition of the audition at Ostia, when he heard God's voice without mediation. God's eternity and immortality were then disclosed. Moreover, the impassibility of the divine will was also made clear to him. These are the foundations of his concept of God as he begins to conceptualize tentatively what is beyond any comprehensive finite representation. Notice that these aspects of God – eternity, immortality, impassibility – are not so much qualitative characterizations as exclusions – of time, mortality and change. They help to locate God at the apex of the hierarchy of reality. This larger metaphysical understanding of God comes into greater focus as Augustine continues to explain what was disclosed to him (*Confessions* XII.11.11):

> Moreover you have spoken to me, Lord, with a strong voice in my inner ear, that you have made all natures and substances which are not what you are and yet exist. And only that which is not from you does not exist. And the motion of the will away from you, who does exist, towards that which exists to a lesser degree, is a fault and a sin. And no one's sin either harms you or disturbs the order of your rule, whether first or last. In your sight this is clear to me; may it be more and more clear, I pray you, and in this manifestation may I abide with surety beneath your wings.

Here we discover once again the reality of God as the productive source of all things. In the second Ostian narrative, those were the things that exclaimed: 'We did not make ourselves, but he made us who abides in eternity.' There is nothing else existing outside of God's creation, in particular no independent power of evil. As in *Confessions* VII, the disclosure of the absolute reality of God brings with it the recognition that evil is the motion of the will away from God. But even so, that contrary motion does not destroy the goodness and order of creation – something we will need to return to in Chapter 4.

Yet it was vitally important for Augustine's Catholic understanding of God to insist that the divine creation of finite things was not itself the cause of evil. The production of a reality distinct from God and invested with volition was not, in itself, a culpable departure away from God. It was the exercise of that volition to separate from God in the interest of self-autonomy that occasioned evil. What makes that evident is the existence of the first level of transcendent creation, the heaven of heaven. Here Augustine turns to a biblical image, a conflation of the 'heaven' produced by God in Gen. 1.1 with the 'heaven of heaven' mentioned in Ps. 113.16. On this spiritual reading, these phrases point to a transcendent heaven, a spiritual heaven beyond the physical heaven, a first product of God that emerges prior to the earthly level of creation. That is the insight disclosed to him: the existence of a spiritual level of reality made up of created beings who exercise a collective decision to remain in immediate association with God. They form a transcendent society, a community immediately participating in God. They have individual volition, but they remain jointly centred on the divine Wisdom. Besides 'heaven of heaven', he also calls this spiritual community the 'house of God' and the 'heavenly Jerusalem'.

This first level of creation is not, strictly speaking, eternal, as only God is eternal, but neither is it in the stream of time. Here is how Augustine describes it (*Confessions* XII.11.12):

> Moreover you have spoken to me, Lord, with a strong voice in my inner ear, that this creature whose delight is you alone, is not coeternal with you. And with a persevering purity it draws itself to you and never betrays its mutability on any occasion. For you are always present to it, and it holds onto you with its total affection. Having no future to expect and not passing into the remembered past, it is altered by no change and is not distended into the succession of time.

The language here resonates with the description of contemplation at Ostia. The heaven of heaven is a creature of God generated to contemplate him. It is free from the sequence of earthly time – especially the division of time into past, present and future. But it is, nevertheless, not eternal as is the Trinity. Because it can be described as persisting in its unmediated contemplation of God, the heaven of heaven has some residual sense of temporality associated with it. It is a creature whose love of God is said to preclude its falling away into the distension of earthly time. That notion of distension was featured in Augustine's meditation on time in *Confessions* XI. There he describes time as a distension of the mind, a state of anxiety that defines the human condition. Indeed, he regards his life as a distension that he wishes to resolve into the stability of eternity (*Confessions* XI.29.39):

> Now my years pass in groans but you, Lord, are my consolation, and my eternal father. I am broken into moments whose order I do not understand, and turbulent shifts rend my thoughts – the inmost entrails of my soul, – until cleansed and purified by the fire of your love, I flow into you.

That moment of understanding at Ostia anticipated this final state of union. The heavenly Jerusalem is the transcendent station to which his soul and Monica's ascended and from which they were drawn into that instance of direct association with the divine Wisdom. This becomes even clearer as his description of it dovetails with the language of the Ostian narrative (*Confessions* XI.13.16):

> So in the meantime my understanding is that the heaven of heaven is an intellectual heaven, where the intellect knows simultaneously, not in part, not in an enigma, not through a mirror, but completely, openly, face to face. This knowing is not of one thing now and then of another, but – as has been said – simultaneous and without any temporal alteration.

One of the most powerful and pervasive themes in the writings of Augustine is the image of exile and return. It has its roots precisely here, in the experience of transcendence that convinced him that there exists an eternal God, and, moreover, that it is the human soul's destiny to flow back into union with God. That is why Augustine characteristically writes as a pilgrim soul rather than an outside observer. He believes he has been there, at the level of perfect and stable reality which was the intended place for human souls before the fall and the only place which might offer rest to the soul. This too is why the scriptures are so critical for him. They offer a medium provided by God to direct the soul towards its source. In a telling remark, Augustine refers to Moses as the author of Genesis, and he says: 'Moses wrote this, he wrote it and went off, crossing hence from you to you' (*Confessions* XI.3.5). That is the story of human beings for Augustine. We are from God and pass through this world on a journey we may hope will unite us with our eternal author. To make sense of that path through the anxieties of time, the scriptures offer sacred disclosures to orient and direct the soul. The sacred texts offer what are often earthly and temporal stories and images, when read literally. But they harbour a deeper power, meeting the soul in its fractured and distended state by directing it to its transcendent home. This is what the scriptures opened up for Augustine in the case of the vision at Ostia, a frame of conceptual reference and a warrant for transcendence, both human and divine.

# Contemplation and the God of Augustine

That 'moment of understanding' at Ostia defined the subsequent spiritual life of Augustine. How could it not have? He insists that that his soul and Monica's came into unmediated association with divine Wisdom. Thereafter, Augustine was a man consumed with longing for a return to that momentary intimation of eternity. Yet, while contemplation of God at Ostia was defined by the silence of all speech and the inadequacy of every sign, nevertheless Augustine's soul turned back into the transitory world of discourse. How then did Augustine go on to describe God after Ostia?

An answer to that question can be found in the prologue to the *Confessions* where Augustine invites God to disclose how to call upon him. He offers a long meditation on what he understands God to be, much as we saw in the *Soliloquies*. Here we can see how Augustine regards scripture as the revealed means that offers fallen humanity both a provisional representation of God within finite, temporal discourse, and a sketch to direct the soul's return to eternity. Scripture opens to the soul both a path beyond the scattered patterns of fallen earthly life, with its anxieties and moral confusions, and a power to recover the soul's immortal destiny. It is, above all, eschatological in nature: instructing, directing, admonishing towards a higher end. What it does not do is appraise the transcendent God from afar and offer a finite, literal portrait of God. That would be to mistake its character as an icon for an idol. As Augustine warns his opponents in *Confessions* XII, scripture may be open to several levels of meaning, but its purpose is, in the end, salvific. It is revelation whose purpose is the recovery of souls, not the conceptual description of God. To settle for a literal reading of scripture is to confirm the soul's distance from God and to underscore its absence from his presence. That is a misunderstanding of the nature of revelation. Scripture should instead be understood to be medicinal, treating the anxieties of temporality and directing the soul's return to God.

There is no better place to observe this than the outset of the *Confessions*. Let's look at the famous first paragraph, which if read closely, explains the purpose of human discourse about God (*Confessions* I.1.1):

> You are great, Lord, and highly to be praised; your power is mighty and your wisdom incalculable. Yet humanity, a tiny

part of your creation, desires to praise you – while bearing its
mortality, bearing witness to its sin, and bearing witness that
you resist the proud. Nonetheless humanity, a tiny part of your
creation, desires to praise you. You stir us up to delight in praising
you, since you made us for yourself, and our hearts are restless
until they rest in you.

That last phrase about the restless heart is perhaps the most
famous quote from the *Confessions*. But we need to be clear what
Augustine is really claiming here as he announces the theme of
his autobiography. He is not saying that humans have an inherent
homing instinct that naturally directs us to God. Rather, humans
are a ruined species, confused, lacking in wisdom and powerless to
achieve the stability of eternity on their own. We bear about us our
mortality because our self-orientation, our pride defines us. But God
stirs our souls to recognize the creative power and infinite wisdom
upon which our finite existence depends. Little bits of creation that
we are, we nonetheless receive the capacity to recognize both our
finitude and our infinite divine source. To praise God is to take
delight in existence and in its foundation, something that is only
possible when human consciousness is directed beyond the buzz
of earthly life. Then the soul can turn towards eternal beauty and
goodness, and restore a relationship with its creator. To do so is to
shift our moral centre away from ourselves and towards the true
centre of our existence. Thus, pride is the original sin for Augustine:
a separation from God initiated by the soul as its turns towards
itself and invests itself with a misplaced sense of independence.
It values its own existence and loses sight of its contingency. The
soul's pride thus initiates the anxiety of its temporal existence, from
which it desires relief. That is the rest that the soul seeks when
stirred by God. To achieve it, the soul must praise God, for to do
so is turn out of itself and back towards its source. Doing so begins
the restoration of an immediate relationship with God, which is its
original, created condition intended by God.

Augustine returned to this theme at the conclusion of the
*Confessions* (XIII.37.51-53). Meditating on God's rest on the
seventh day of creation in Genesis, Augustine describes how we may
hope to rest in God, who will then also rest in us. But this does not
mean that God changes, he says, for God is outside time. Thinking
in such terms is the result of our projection of earthly discourse

onto God. Instead, the rest of God can only be grasped by the soul who is admitted into the presence of God, who rests in God and God in him. Only in the Wisdom of God can true understanding be found, not at a distance, not through the teaching of angels or human wisdom. It is with that echo of Ostia that the *Confessions* concludes. Here are its final lines:

> Yet you, the good, are in need of no other good, and so are forever at peace. Since you are peace itself, you are peace. But who can give to another human the ability to understand this? And which angel can give to another this ability? Which angel can give this to a human? Yet you can be begged, you can be asked, you can be banged on. Yes, that is how it is grasped, how it is discovered, how it is revealed.

True knowledge of God is, therefore, only possible when God opens the door of transcendence to the soul. Then the soul's self-inflicted separation from God can be reversed and God discerned without the barriers of time and space, immediately and without mediation. This point is of the utmost importance for reading Augustine. It follows from those transcendental experiences that first confirmed to him with absolute certainty the existence of God, a truth more certain than his own existence. The knowledge of God that Augustine and Monica acquired at Ostia was described as an anticipation of the eschatological state of their souls. Then, after death, the soul would enter the heavenly Jerusalem and join the life of the saints, abiding in contemplative union with the divine Wisdom. But now we can only strive to achieve that state, as Monica did throughout her life, by praising God and following the path defined by the community of saints on earth, the church. Now our knowledge of God is perforce fragmentary, temporally bound and warped by the self-orientation that is the root of our fallen condition. It is, above all, a distanced appraisal, subject to the distortions of perspective and prism of our earthly condition. We must, in consequence, not mistake the claims we make about God out of the opacity of time, space and finitude, as binding truth claims. That is the folly of cognitive pride. But we can nonetheless anticipate that higher, eschatological knowledge of God when we undertake to follow patterns of wisdom offered in God's self-revelation. There, in the scriptures, divine disclosure can be found, one that dovetails with contemplative revelation.

Together these two sources offer the soul a sketch for its return to God – a map not a picture, an icon not an idol. The ineffable immediacy of contemplation is given a limited conceptual frame, consistent with the soul's present earthly condition. But finite discourse about the infinite and transcendent God is a concession, not to be mistaken for formal description. To do so would be to freeze the soul at its current spiritual distance from God, to settle for accuracy rather than intimacy.

With this caveat in mind, we can turn now to *Confessions* I, where Augustine ask this question: 'So who are you, my God?' This is an instance of what might be called the vocative dimension of prayer, something that frames the whole of the *Confessions*. He uses this rhetorical mode for a specific purpose. Whatever he says descriptively about God folds into an extended discourse directed to God. Thus, Augustine is describing God while seeking to deepen his soul's association with him. What he says follows directly from his experiences of contemplation and is phrased in light of the transcendence of God discovered in those episodes. Augustine is thus acutely aware of the paradox involved in speaking about God. He discerned in contemplation that there is no privileged vantage point from which to observe a transcendent God. Nor is there any way to stand apart from an omnipresent God. Moreover, how can he ask God to come to him in prayer, since God's presence is a precondition of his being? There is, in a sense, a specious sense of distance involved in any discourse directed to God or describing God. For Augustine has discovered the transcendent root of his soul in divine being (*Confessions* I.2.2):

> I would not have existed, my God, I would not have existed at all, if you were not in me. Or, to put it best, I would not have existed unless I existed in you, from whom are all things, and through whom are all things, and in whom are all things.

That last phrase is an echo of Rom. 11.36. So whether describing or invoking God, the soul seeks to recover and intensify a latent divine presence at its core. Discourse about God must support that goal, not frustrate it.

But something must nonetheless be said about God while the soul is on its journey through time. Augustine offers his readers in the *Confessions* his own account, a diffident set of conceptual pointers to direct the soul in its efforts to deepen communion with God already inchoately sensed. Following the practice we have already observed, Augustine uses scriptural concepts to express his new Christian understanding of God. He begins by setting out a series of superlatives: most high, most good, most powerful, most omnipotent. These terms make several things clear about the God of Ostia. God is the absolute reality, above and beyond all else things in his being. As the One God there is no other power commensurate or rivalling him. Moreover, God is superlative in an evaluative sense: completely good. All these superlatives elaborate the transcendent God encountered at Ostia. They point beyond any treatment of God as finite or bound within space and time.

Then Augustine amplifies divine transcendence with a long list of paired conceptions – sometimes contrasting and even paradoxical – designed to press the soul beyond the standard range of its earthly understanding and to direct it towards God. God is described as (*Confessions* I.4.4):

> most merciful and most just,
> most separate yet most present,
> most beautiful and strongest,
> stable but endless,
> immutable but changing all things,
> never old, never new,
> making everything old, yet leading the proud unknowingly to
>   be old,
> always active, always at rest,
> collecting, but without needing,
> carrying and filling and protecting,
> creating and nurturing and completing,
> searching, though for you nothing is missing.

Augustine then reaffirms the vocative dimension, restoring direct address (*Confessions* I.4.4):

> You love without wavering,
> You are jealous, but without being troubled,
> You repent without being sorry,
> You are wrathful but tranquil,
> You change things without changing your intent,

You take back what you find, but had never lost,
You are never lacking, yet you rejoice in gains,
You are never avaricious, yet you weigh your interest,
We overpay you so that you might be indebted to us,
but who has anything that is not yours?
You repay debts, though owing no one,
You cancel debts, but lose nothing.

Augustine pointedly concludes with another reminder of the
inadequacy of divine description: 'But what have I said, my God,
my life, my sacred sweetness? Or rather, what has anyone said
when he speaks of you?' (Confessions I.4.4). This reference to holy
sweetness points to his continuing sense of the divine presence
in his soul. That sweetness is the contemporaneous awareness of
God continuing within his soul, the living residue of Ostia. What
this exercise in words about God is meant to achieve is a similar,
magnified sense of the God beyond space and time, but present even
now as the reality upon which the soul's existence rests.

    This presence disclosed in contemplation had a final aspect
that we need to consider, and that is divine love. That is the third
aspect of God that he offers his readers in the initial account of
his enlightenment (Confessions VII.10.16), along with 'eternal
truth' and 'beloved eternity'. While those terms point towards
God's transcendence, 'true love' underscores God's pervasive
attention within the soul. Here we come to the source of that great
Augustinian theme: divine omnipresence. Augustine emerged from
that instance of enlightenment with an overwhelming conviction of
God's immediate presence, not just in all elements of reality, but most
acutely in the interior depth of the human soul. There are several
dimensions of this insight that jump out from his efforts to sketch
this idea. First, God is conscious of human individuals in their core
of their being. The web of his presence is not just ontological but
intellective. More than just the sustainer of all things in existence,
God is cognizant of them as they are in themselves. Thus, God is
omnipresent consciousness and the reality that he knows includes
his creation, not just himself. Moreover, Augustine has discerned a
twofold pattern, as it were, in the inner life of God. God's goodness
overflows in an act of self-diffusion, which is creation. And then
God draws all things back towards God in an expression of love.
The divine agency of creation is counterpoised by the magnetism of

grace. That deep cosmic rhythm is a free expression of God's own reality, not an automatic process. It is an act of love both in the bestowal of the gift of finite existence and in the enfolding of the soul back into the immediacy of the divine presence. This, Augustine believes, was revealed to him in that instant of contemplation. For this reason the idea of God's conscious presence in the soul became one of the central themes of the *Confessions*. That work is not so much an autobiography as a fragmentary expression of self-awareness offered in the conscious presence of God. The transcendence of God disclosed to him was but one mode of the divine life, balanced the love of God for individual created beings.

To grasp this vast contemplative understanding of God more fully, we need to turn now to Augustine's treatment of the human soul. That will help us come to terms more clearly with the nature of the self and the process of its spiritual return to its source.

# 3

# The Soul

*I had become a great question to myself*

'A ghost in a machine.' That is how the soul is sometimes described. The phrase accentuates a jarring inconsistency between an occult substance and the physical body that contains it. It was Gilbert Ryle, the British philosopher, who came up this pithy formula, part of his critique of modern mind/body dualism (Ryle 1949). Some ancient philosophers thought like this as well, producing works on the soul as if it were an invisible substance. Among them was the young Augustine, who wrote a treatise right after his conversion in 386/7 entitled *On the Immortality of the Soul*. When he went back to read it late in his life (426/7), he found it incomprehensible (*Reconsiderations* 1.5.1). In the intervening years he broadened the range of his thinking, since he found classical accounts of the soul inadequate to capture the Christian enlightenment that had transformed his life.

That is because his vision of God had been self-reflexive. It had not just disclosed the absolute reality of God, it had confronted him with his own moral state. And that was painful and ugly. His interior experience of transcendence had opened and closed in an instant, and it had occurred only through divine assistance. He realized then that this inner aperture to the divine was closed off by the moral detritus of the soul's fall, by refractory moral forces that dwelt deep down within. And so in that moment of transformative disclosure in Milan he became acutely aware of the moral depravity of his soul. There lay the painful paradox of transcendence for Augustine. In finding God he discovered his own spiritual poverty. Moreover, by confronting the story of his pride and self-deception, a deeper self was disclosed, one which was capable of moral self-recognition, even if it was incapable of changing its own ethical condition.

This chapter will trace the informal logic of the soul in Augustine. Once again our focus will be on the conversionary Augustine, the Augustine who expanded his conceptual palette beyond traditional philosophy in an effort to sort out what he had discovered in contemplation. In doing so we can observe him exercising what might be called confessional introspection in order to come to terms with the limits of contemplation. That process of self-interrogation is the *Confessions*.

## Confessional Introspection

Introspection was the way Augustine discovered God. Yet, while introspection was essential, it was not sufficient to secure the soul's immediate knowledge of God on its own. You can see this if you go back and take a second look at the three ascension narratives – the two pre-baptismal accounts from book VII in Chapter 1 and the vision at Ostia from book IX in Chapter 2. Several things are made quite evident in these texts about the nature and power of the soul.

First, all of these ascents occur – as Augustine says – 'in the presence of truth' and that truth is Christ, the divine Wisdom. Although his consciousness shifts through various interior levels, what he discovers is not a subjective image of reality, but truth itself. This means that the immanent presence of God in the soul opens into recognition of divine transcendence, the absolute reality of God. Failure to attend to the interior presence of God leads us into confusion and, paradoxically, foreshortens our ability to grasp objective truth. The purpose of the interior turn is to drill down into the depth of the self, to the point where the self discerns the transcendent source of its own being. By going within itself, the soul discovers what it has hitherto missed, the neglected presence of God without which it would not exist.

Second, all three ascension narratives emphasize that the soul makes this interior ascension because of divine assistance. This point is made unmistakably clear. In the initial narrative of *Confessions* VII.10.16, Augustine underscores that it is God's assistance that gives him the power to enter the inner chamber of his soul. In

*Confessions* VII.17.23 his soul is drawn up by divine beauty but comes crashing back to ordinary consciousness because of the weight of its unruly passions. At Ostia in *Confessions* IX.10.23-25, the souls of Monica and her son are lifted up by the power of divine love. These extraordinary moments of consciousness became for Augustine the basis for his theology of the human soul. From them he composed a general principle that would anchor his subsequent thinking: that the soul is not in command of its own spiritual destiny.

There are two reasons for this defining judgement on the nature of the human soul. Just before the second account of his enlightenment, Augustine foreshadows to his readers what he will come to discover (*Confessions* VII.15.21–16.22). First, God alone is infinite, eternal and real, while all other things are finite, temporal and parasitic in their existence. There is, then, a bright line of separation between a human soul and its permanently abiding source. As such, the soul cannot be mistaken for an immortal being; it is not divine, and it lacks the power to cross that barrier between time and eternity on its own. Second, souls have been deformed by the rebellion of the human race, by the fall of human soul from its initially perfect status. This larger thesis Augustine has gleaned from the story of Adam and Eve, who represent all humanity (*Confessions* X.22.29). He believed that a deep perversity had led humans to compound their contingent natures by separating themselves from God. What began as a natural distinction between the infinite and the finite mushroomed into a painful estrangement from the beautiful and the good. Here is how he explains this in *Confessions* VII.16.22:

> And I questioned what iniquity was, and I did not find a substance but instead the perversity of a twisted will deviating from the highest substance, which is you, O God, towards inferior things, abandoning itself and swelling out.

Little wonder then that the soul is powerless to reassert its connection to God, having lost its proper nature and become deeply enmeshed in space and time.

This is why contemplative introspection was painfully reflexive for Augustine. His soul was now a twisted substance, different from the perfection of its original state. In being lifted up to eternal being, his soul was forced to confront both its contingent nature, and more painful still, the effects of its fall. In those moments of contemplative introspection, God had conferred on him momentarily a spiritual vantage point that his soul did not merit. What is striking is that this is true of the pre-baptismal accounts as well the post-baptismal episode at Ostia. Contingency and the effects of the fall have not been obviated by his new Christian life. A hard road of prayer and discipline lay ahead, for his enlightenment only initiated a process of spiritual renewal, it did not accomplish it. This is where 'confessional introspection' comes in, the radical spiritual self-analysis that Augustine exercises in the *Confessions* (Stern-Gillet 2006; Kenney 2006). It might seem natural that moral introspection would lead to confession, and then expiation of sin would then result in enlightenment. But for Augustine that pattern is wrong and needs to be reversed. It assumes the potential success of ethical self-discernment and a human capacity for achieving moral lucidity. Yet Augustine's own experience has led him to reject that possibility. He came to believe that the effects of the fall have left the human soul with a refractory moral consciousness, deeply prone to self-deception. Pride and self-centredness are so embedded in the present human condition that moral introspection is doomed to failure. He has the story of his life to prove all this. Only the power of Christ, given as a free gift, can offer restoration to his soul. And only then is the soul capable of genuinely honest introspection. His extraordinary moments of enlightenment were instances of that power, of what became known as 'grace'. If it was true for him, it was true for everyone.

In the aftermath of those exceptional moments of contemplative introspection, he set about the practice of confessional introspection, of serious moral self-editing. This he now regarded as integral to a Christian life. It is easy to see why this should be so. He had been shown the abiding paradox of the human condition: the latent presence in the soul of divine being, sustaining his existence, while he remained in a 'region of dissimilarity', estranged from his true self and his creator. Moreover, he was a mortal creature. He had only a limited time to deal with his spiritual state, for his soul was not divine and could not anticipate successive reincarnations, as the Platonists believed. Thus, the temporal frame of this mortal existence became absolutely critical: he had but one life to sort things out spiritually. And he had already lived beyond the average life expectancy in the ancient world; indeed, within five years of his conversion, he would bury both his mother and his adolescent son. Compounding these problems were the moral failures of his past, the addictive passions that had overwhelmed him, the subtle warping of his judgement by his education in classical pagan culture, his obsession with fame and power. He regarded himself as enslaved and helpless.

Yet the power that flooded his soul at his conversion was, he believed, available to him still, the power of Christ. As he says so many times in his writings, Christ is the inner physician of the soul. That is what had happened to him one day in the summer of 386 when, seated in a garden in Milan, he had heard the voices of children chanting repeatedly 'take up and read'. So picking up the epistles of Paul, he read Rom. 13.13-14, a passage exactly attuned to his impoverished moral state: 'Not in reveling and drunkenness, not in debauchery and sexual excess, not in strife and envy, but put on the Lord Jesus Christ, and make no provision for the flesh in its lusts.' He then says that a light of relief flooded his heart, and all anxiety and doubt dissipated (*Confessions* VIII.12.29). That was no coincidence. It was the power of Christ drawing his soul by the magnetism of grace at a crucial moment of personal anxiety and despair. It was a breakthrough of divine grace, one that Augustine believed had been prepared by Christ throughout his life, present always but ignored. Going forward as a Christian, he must now routinize that salvific presence.

He described this ignored presence of divine beauty in one of the most powerful passages in the *Confessions* X.27.38:

> Late have I loved you, beauty so old and so new, late have I loved you. And behold, you were within me and I was outside myself, and I sought you there, and thus impaired I threw myself into those beautiful things that you had made. You were with me but I was not with you. Those beautiful things kept me far from you, though they would not exist if they did not exist in you. You called out and shouted and destroyed my deafness. You gleamed and were radiant and drove away my blindness. You were fragrant and I inhaled and panted after you. I tasted you and I hunger and thirst for you. You touched me, and I burn for your peace.

There is urgency and regret here. Notice the paradox of presence: Beauty, the power of divine creation, had always been with him, sustaining his existence, but ignored by him. The beautiful things of the material world, however good in themselves, had become for him a distracting impediment. But the force of immaterial beauty shattered his nescience. Yet he was still living among the things of this world. Now he needed to live so that he remained conscious of the presence of divine beauty, without distraction by those lovely created things. The peace of that transcendent state must be cultivated and secured within temporal life.

To do so he needed divine help, both to continue to control his passions and to understand how he had failed in the past and even now continued to do so. His experiences of enlightenment were, he now realized, as much disclosures of God's omnipresence within his soul as of God's transcendence. That presence had been there throughout his entire life, he had just failed to notice. Now he got it. The mess he had made of his life brought him to a crisis and weakened his ability to block out the divine presence at the core of his soul. This was the voice of the sustainer of his existence. So his enlightenment had not been a change of his nature. He had not been struck blind or visited by angels. There was no external drama; the drama was all within himself. There he discovered the God who had been within him all along. Now he had to figure out how to draw upon that inner power and to secure that state of serenity both now and into eternity.

Anxieties about how he could really live this new life turn up from the first works he wrote after his conversion. So too does his faith in the inner presence of Christ. We can see this in *Soliloquies* – a work we looked at earlier – written just after his enlightenment experience in Milan and before his baptism. There is a fascinating passage in *Soliloquies* 1.22, where Augustine is having an introspective discussion with Reason. Reason describes Augustine as a would-be philosopher, a lover of Wisdom or Sophia:

> Now we might ask what sort of lover of wisdom you are. You desire to see and to hold her, with an entirely pure glance and in an embrace without a veil in between, naked as it were, which she allows only to the very few and most select of her lovers.

Wisdom surrenders herself only to the lover who is exclusively devoted to her, not to those who are feckless and still enthralled by lesser objects of desire. Purity of intention is required to sustain such a love of wisdom for her own sake. The language of unveiled union with Wisdom resonates with the initial descriptions of contemplation in *Confessions* VII, as does the light imagery that follows (*Soliloquies* 1.23):

> That is just how lovers of wisdom should be. She seeks those whose union with her is pure and without defilement. But there is more than just one way to her. Indeed each one grasps that unique and most true good according to health and strength. This light of our minds is ineffable and incomprehensible. The ordinary light shows us, as much as possible, how that other light exists.

That light of our minds is ineffable. All souls must ultimately turn for enlightenment to that light which is ineffable and beyond description or comprehension. But the soul requires divine aid to turn to the ineffable light. Beauty then reveals herself when the soul is ready. Indeed, beauty serves as a physician to the soul (*Soliloquies* 1.25):

> That beauty knows, however, when to reveal itself. So it functions as a physician, and it knows better those who are healthy than those who are being treated.

This early passage dovetails with the later account on divine beauty from *Confessions* X, just quoted above. Both texts describe the latent presence of divine beauty within the soul. That beauty breaks through into the soul's consciousness and, by this act of self-revelation, transforms it. That moment is medicinal, beginning to cure the soul of its misplaced love for the contingent things of this world. This image, of a divine physician treating the misplaced passions of the fallen soul, became a dispositive theme for Augustine. It helped him articulate the central need for souls to believe in Christ, who alone had the power to cure. He insists in *Confessions* VI.4.6 that his soul could only be healed if he trusted the healing hands of Christ:

> I could have been cured by believing, so that my mind's eye, once purified, might have been directed to some degree towards your truth that remains forever and never wanes. But just as it often

happens that someone who has experienced a bad physician fears trusting himself to a good one, so it was with the sickness of my soul. It certainly could not be healed except by believing, yet it refused to be cured for fear of believing false things. It resisted your hands, though you had prepared the medicines of faith, and sprinkled them upon the sicknesses of the world, and granted such power to them.

Those medicines of faith are the practices of the Christian life. They open the eye of the soul and allow it to see itself without fevered images.

Confessional introspection is, therefore, possible only for souls who have come to recognize that inner divine presence and have come to believe in Christ. Christ, he says, was the 'physician of my most intimate self' (*Confessions* X.3.4). Yet only Christian souls can avail themselves of his healing power. This point is of the utmost importance for reading Augustine. He is not recommending to his readers introspection for its own sake. That had not worked for him. His Christian enlightenment showed him the way he would need to follow to achieve spiritual peace. His past efforts to know himself had led to moral impasse and personal breakdown. If that ancient Delphic admonition – to know oneself – was to be accomplished, it would only be through a gift of God. This is because the human soul is just too weak to know itself, to come to terms with the dark forces that the fall of Adam and Eve had unleashed. Philosophers like the Platonists have largely missed this point. Correct on divine transcendence, they misunderstood the fallen nature of the soul. Though noble in its capacity to contemplate the transcendent to some degree, Augustine had discovered that the 'darknesses' of human soul restricted its spiritual capacities (*Confessions* VII.20.26). Platonists taught that the soul could indeed know itself as divine and discern the root of the Good within the soul. But they were wrong. Here Augustine introduced the title theme of the *Confessions*, contrasting the presumption of the philosophers with the confession practised by Christians in their humility. It was their recognition of the limits of the soul's power that set Christians apart.

In the first sections of *Confessions* X, Augustine explains why he is writing his autobiography. It is an exercise in confessional introspection, an effort to know himself through the light of Christ now dwelling within him. Moreover, he is modelling this practice for other Christians. He also explains the Christian search for self-knowledge, riffing off a series of embedded texts from Genesis, Isaiah and I and II Corinthians. The passage is worth quoting in full. Notice that it is the immutability of God that offers surety to the soul, in contrast to the Manichaean power of Goodness and Light which must passively resist the depredations of Evil and Darkness (*Confessions* X.5.7):

> You, Lord, are my judge. Though no one knows the nature of a person except his inner spirit, yet there is something in each person that even his inner spirit does not know. But you, Lord, know everything about a person, since you made him. Although I despise myself in your sight and judge myself to be dust and ashes, nevertheless I know something of you that I do not know about myself. No doubt we now see through a mirror in an enigma, and not yet face to face. Therefore, as long as I wander from you, I am more present to myself than to you. Yet while I know that you cannot be overcome, I do not know which temptations I can resist and which I cannot. There is hope because you are faithful and will not let us be tempted beyond what we can bear. And in temptation you will give us a way out so we can bear it. Let me confess then what I know of myself. And let me confess what I do not yet know of myself. What I know of myself I know through your light, and what I do not know of myself, I will not know until my darkness is made like noonday before your face.

As pilgrims in this world, nothing is truly clear to us, least of all ourselves. But what we can know is due to the divine light within us. Only that can illumine the opacity of self-presence for the fallen soul. That is why introspection must be conducted in humility and with the guidance of the divine physician. Any introspection that is not confessional is an act of self-aggrandizement, prone to self-deception and an exercise in pride.

## The Cursive Self

Christian introspection is rooted in memory for Augustine. It is the searching of the past that allows the Christian soul to confront the moral failures and deceptive desires that make up any human life conducted in the absence of grace. It also offers the chance to discern the tacit presence of God beneath those chaotic patterns, a source of hidden stability for the soul. Only then, when the past has been interrogated and its conflicting passions have been resolved, can the present be morally assayed and faced with honesty. Much rests on the power of memory for Augustine's account of the Christian soul. The functional importance of memory for Augustine has been well described by philosopher Martha Nussbaum (Nussbaum 2003, 540):

> In Augustine's view, every deed one has ever committed is a deed for which one is going to be judged by God. The Christian, therefore, in order to be maximally able to make an adequate confession, must not be less mindful of his past than another, but more mindful, not less concerned with what his bodily self has done, but more concerned. He must cultivate a very keen sense of his own continuity and unity. He must dredge up the past, rather than severing himself from it.

Dredging up the past as a propaedeutic to the future for the soul now living in Christ. But it is never easy.

This Augustine makes plain in his long meditation on the power of memory in *Confessions* X. There he clarifies both the role of memory and the practice of confessional introspection in his new life as a Christian. His own experiences of contemplative enlightenment were extraordinary but unsustainable. Now he is living the quotidian human struggle against temptation and sin. His Christian readers are doing the same, perhaps absent those moments of union with divine Wisdom that he had experienced, but nonetheless living 'in Christ'. Whereas for him contemplation preceded confessional introspection, now he is back to where all Christians are, practising confessional introspection through divine grace in order to restore union with God. For all Christians that is an eschatological hope, something to be attained after death. He explains how that is now working for him in *Confessions* X. That account follows from many other interior ascension programs that he set out in works written in the decade since his conversion (Kenney 2013).

He begins in *Confessions* X.7.11:

> What then do I love when I love God? Who is he who is higher than the source of my soul? Through my soul itself I will ascend

to him, and rise above the power by which I adhere to the body and fill its frame with vitality. Not by this power can I discover God.

We are back to the ascent at Ostia, but here in an expectant not descriptive voice. Augustine begins with the force within the soul that binds it to the body. Humans and animals both have this capacity. This is the lower function of the soul, the aspect that looks, as it were, downward to the body not upward to God. The same is true of the perceptive faculty of the soul which perceives through the senses. But there is a higher power in the soul that is beyond these natural functions. Augustine says that he will rise step by step to God, and that brings him to 'the fields and vast palaces of memory' (Confessions X.8.12). Here is hidden the record of all our sensory impressions, experiences, actions and so on. Moreover, he tells us that it is searchable on demand, so it is more than just a receptive faculty but an active centre of reflection. Some memories are easy to recover, others flood the mind unexpectedly. Memory is like a huge cavern with mysterious nooks and crannies. He calls it the 'stomach of the mind'. It contains not just sense impressions delivered to the mind in a raw state, but also the impressions that the mind has formed about them. Beyond these are concepts that the mind discovers independent of the senses, including numbers and concepts. So memory encompasses in some respect reason itself. In sum, it is the active seat of self-consciousness.

Here Augustine comes to a crucial point. There is a very real sense in which memory is the function of self-awareness that rides above simple consciousness. As he puts it (Confessions X.15.23):

I name memory and I know what I name. And where do I know this except in memory? Can memory be present to itself through its own image, and not through itself?

This self-reflective autonomy points towards the mind's ability to shift through different mental levels and functions. That capacity is part of the fluidity of consciousness that the soul exhibits, the foundation of its potential of ascent to God. Augustine notes that the memory is able to be conscious of affections and emotions without still experiencing them. It can remember fear, or sadness, or even forgetfulness, without actually exhibiting those states.

That power of reflexive consciousness is the cursive self – mentioned in Chapter 1 – the self that can move over a series of states of consciousness and determine which it chooses. You can see this in his description of the soul's ascent beyond memory (*Confessions* X.17.26):

> What then shall I do, my God, you who are my true life? I will pass beyond this power of mine that is called memory. I will pass beyond that so that I can continue on to you, the sweet light. What are you saying to me? I am ascending through my mind to you, who remains above me. I will pass beyond that power of mine that is called memory, desiring to touch you however you can be touched, and to adhere to you however it is possible to adhere to you.

So the consciousness of the self has moved through various levels of the soul, beginning with the soul's connection to the body. Now it reaches the memory, its principal and most powerful level. It then seeks to move beyond that level in its quest for unity with God. But unless God lifts it up and fills it with the divine presence, it remains what it is at the level of memory. And that means, Augustine tells us, that it will remain a question to itself (*Confessions* X.28.39).

That is a striking and rather odd way to describe the soul's condition. But it is one that he uses several times. In the narrative of the death of his childhood friend, Augustine describes his intense grief (*Confessions* IV.4.9):

> I had become a great question to myself, and I asked my soul: why was it sad and why does it disturb me so intensely? But it did not know what to say to me in response.

Here we have the soul in the grip of inchoate emotions unable to respond to this higher level of consciousness within the self. This capacity to be self-conscious and to exercise a critical awareness of emotional states and moral failures is the cornerstone of confessional introspection. It suggests a promising element of spiritual distance, a measure of perspective that can be sustained and advanced by divine grace. For the fallen soul it is the cause of continuing misery, as this higher level of personal lucidity is overwhelmed by the force of habituation to sin. That condition was described as two competing wills: one distorted by passions and the other only weakly able to recognize the presence of the good (*Confessions* VIII.5.10). But after his conversion, Augustine is able to use this higher consciousness, strengthened by the inner physician, to inspect the state of his soul.

You might expect that all would be well at this stage and that his Christian soul would now be unified in a state of sanctity. But there is no such easy resolution for Augustine. He is surprisingly frank about this. The contemporaneous introspection that he conducts in *Confessions* X yields a mixed report. He now has an increased measure of spiritual strength and serenity that allows the cursive self to identify shortcomings without being dragged down by the chains of habit and ending up out of control. That is why he can write the *Confessions*. But there were still dark recesses of his soul that remain recalcitrant, even after those moments of immediate unity with the divine Wisdom that his soul had enjoyed. For the fall of his soul had left a deeply impacted stratum of resistance to the good. That streak ran so deep it was unconscious. An example he gives is the continuing erotic dreams and fantasies that afflict him. These his reason can resist when awake, but in sleep they elicit his consent and their pleasure seems like the real acts (*Confessions* X.30.41-42). Yet he has come a long way from the days when the 'glue of lust' had left him helpless. Now he has been given the power of conscious control by God, and he anticipates that this control will be extended over his subconscious lusts in the future. He continues this analysis of his mixed moral state at great length, reviewing his level of temptation to excess in music, perfume, food, drink, artistic objects, fame, public spectacles and praise. He is even alert to what he now regards as the temptations of fake religion: magic, astrology and the conjuring of ghosts. As he says: 'We are tempted every day, Lord, tempted without cessation' (*Confessions* X.37.60). Yet he now has some measure of self-control, a conferred ability to rise above the ruts of habit.

We need to think about this cursive self and its larger significance. It is, as we have seen, the aspect of the soul that is strengthened by Christ and has, as it were, the gift of self-perspective. As it becomes more robust, it achieves a tentative sovereignty over the lower elements of the soul. It rides above them in part by its ability to exercise memory, to survey its past deeds and to confront its current dispositions, both conscious and unconscious. In this crucial sense,

the cursive self exhibits an incipient self-transcendence, a capacity
to rise above the level of moral consciousness. In another sense, it
is able to choose the higher levels of the soul, to access its rational
aspect. Moreover, it continues the soul's quest in life to deepen
the presence of God within it. It is here that the salience of the
Christian thought of Augustine becomes particularly evident. In his
assessment of the human condition, Augustine came to believe that
the classical accounts of moral failure were inadequate in numerous
ways. If we think of the choice of evil as a mistake, we assume that
the mind has miscalculated, having decided to do what appeared
good but was, in fact, bad. Yet, the *Confessions* offers a different
perspective, that of weakness of will. Over and over Augustine tells
the tale of his inability to do what he knows is right. He knew
what was right, but he was unable to follow through and do it.
That required God's intervention in his life, something that must be
continuous. When he speaks of grace in this way, it might sometime
sound as if he thinks of it as a divine additive designed to strengthen
the will.

But far more is involved. First, he thinks that the will is not just
flawed and, at times, ineffectual, he regards it as corrupted. We have
already seen that language of a twisted and corrupt will. Indeed,
on his Pauline account of human nature, the fall of humanity has
left our souls in behavioural chains that are perverse and seemingly
inexorable. They are rooted in the deep soul, which as we just saw,
includes unconscious dispositions and propensities. Moreover, there
is a collective dimension to sin, for our souls are acculturated to
choose many things that are evil, even if their conventional nature
blunts that recognition. Augustine spends much of the earlier books
of the *Confessions* cataloguing the misguided choices he made in his
early life, many of which were highly regarded or at least acceptable
within his society. These include his rhetorical career itself, his
classical education in pagan literature, his taking a concubine, his
obsession with the theatre, his ambitious and relentless pursuit of
fame and social standing and so forth. These were not the result of
weakness of will but of the will's wholesale perversion. Here was
deeply impacted social evil, pursued in a state of moral nescience.
His own story was the choice of many socially sanctioned choices
and approved goods which left him, nonetheless, miserable and
morally impoverished. He came to regard evil as vast and systemic,
part of the architecture of the fallen world. As such it was insidious.

It was far more than a rational miscalculation, and even more than just a matter of weakness of the will. It was a collective catastrophe in which our souls are endlessly mired and inchoately complicit.

For the soul to choose the good, it must become good. And to do that it needs to achieve some measure of self-perspective. That is where that higher self comes in, the self that could begin to recognize that he had begun to be a question to himself. That voice over and above the narrative of immediate consciousness offers a wedge against complete immersion the things of this world. If the higher soul can ride above its confusions, even if only by recognizing them to be such, it can begin to find a way out. That is what the inner presence of God in the soul offers. God is omnipresent within the soul, and that force calls the soul above passions, dispositions and cultural perversities. To recognize that divine presence and to follow its inner voice is to restore a connection to the good itself. It is to be 'in Christ', entering into the valence of divine love that made the soul and seeks its return. It is that power alone that can resist the deep patterns of evil that make up the architecture of the fallen world. When Augustine spoke of God as 'eternal truth and true love and beloved eternity', this is, in part, what he meant.

He knew that this divine power was real because it allowed his higher soul to loosen the chains of evil. This was more than just a strengthening of the will, it was a profound transformation. It was not, however complete, as the inventory of temptation indicates. For all life in the world remains conditioned by the fall. But being in communion with Christ can offer that inner lucidity that permits the soul to choose the good and to achieve some measure of purity of heart. Augustine tells us that even amid his temptations he still has intimations of contemplation. That is the inner presence of God manifesting itself within the higher soul. He describes this in similar terms twice in *Confessions* X. Here is the first of these from *Confessions* X.6.8:

> Yet I love a certain light and a certain voice and a certain fragrance and a certain food and a certain embrace when I love my God. Light, voice, food, embrace of my inner self, where light shines into my soul that no space can contain, where sound resonates that no time can dissipate, where fragrance permeates that no breeze can disperse, where taste is savored that no eating can

diminish, where there is a union that no satiety can sunder – that is what I love when I love my God.

The second passage is from *Confessions* X.40.65:

Sometimes you admit me into an unusual state within myself of such unknown sweetness. If it were perfected in me, I do not know what the future life will be that this state is not. But I fall back again under those wretched weights and am reabsorbed by my usual habits.

Both texts describe not the transcendent union with God as at Ostia, but a continuing presence of God within the innermost soul that permeates it. The soul is ennobled by the divine light that coexists together with evil dispositions within the soul. As in all such texts, Augustine underscores the catalytic character of the divine presence. For the omniscient God is alert to the struggles of the higher self with inchoate forces within the soul. It needs these manifestations of divine presence to lift the higher soul beyond its lower elements. Those drag it down into the outer world and rob it of its inherent spiritual nature. Intimations of contemplative union, of a restored bond of union with God, support the higher soul as it sorts out the problems of its fallen existence. But God is immediately cognizant that, in its fallen state, its current condition is perplexing to itself. Without divine direction, there would be no hope that the soul's limited self-reflective power could lead it to God. Only the medicinal presence of Christ can accomplish that.

# Transcendence of the Soul

'In your eyes I have become a great question to myself, and that is my illness' (*Confessions* X.33.50; cf. IV.4.9 quoted above). That is an odd thing to say, but if you think about it, you can model what Augustine means here. He is capable of sufficient self-reflection to acknowledge his lifetime of bad choices and addictive behaviours. Yet he was miserable not just because he is suffering the consequences of his actions. His sickness was a function both of his being out of control and also of his intense awareness of that condition. It was the latter that was especially painful, though it was also the deeply revealing. Augustine was morally miserable precisely because he could discern his situation. In this respect he had achieved something like God's perspective. And that was a small, initial act of self-transcendence.

It was the higher soul, the cursive self, which accomplished this. In this respect the long narrative of Augustine's moral wanderings in the *Confessions* supports one essential fact: the self-reflexive character of the soul signals its transcendence of the material world. Because he could tell his story, he was not just another mammal. Nor was that moral self-consciousness adequately described as an occult substance in a body, 'a ghost in a machine'. The self-consciousness that could be aware of his life's experiences from the inside out had to be more than just some sort of physical substance, whether material or occult. His self-reflection was an activity that betokened an element of himself that went deeper than that. This element made it possible for him to be both ethically responsible and morally frustrated. And it also disclosed an openness to something beyond itself, to the root of its being and the source of its moral renewal.

That self-reflexive power within was what he meant by soul. It was best understood as immaterial in character. It was a self-reflective consciousness that counterbalanced the desires of the flesh, expressing a centripetal longing for the divine core of reality. For Augustine, to be human is to be caught between desire for the lovely things of the temporal world and an inchoate longing for their eternal source. The principal problem of embodied life was to discover a higher identity – to secure communion with the divine Wisdom. Only then could life in the world be possible without dispersion in temporal passions which are beneath the dignity of a transcendent soul. Yet moral distraction always remains a danger. But the soul who had discovered the inner physician and had begun to be cured was a soul no longer ignorant of its true identity, no longer mistaken about its transcendent destiny.

That transcendent prospect for the soul is in many ways essential for what Augustine understood the soul to be. Far from being a bit of ghostly stuff captured in a body – a Manichaean image – the soul was the point of intersection between time and eternity. That was, in a sense, the source of his disquietude throughout his earlier life. Absent this intimation of a more perfect reality, he would not have been so dissatisfied with the finite pleasures and goods to which he had devoted himself. He illuminates this seam in the structure of reality in *Confessions* XI and XII and helps us see the larger meaning of 'soul'. There he lays out a level of reality that is comprised of intelligent beings, of souls, that transcend space and time. This is the first creation of God and the goal that embodied souls seek after their earthly lives. We first encountered this conception in Chapter 2. He calls it the heaven of heaven, that is, the transcendent heaven beyond the physical heaven of the cosmos. It is a collective entity made up of souls who form a community engaged in unmediated contemplation of God. It was this contemplative community that he and Monica had joined in that instant at Ostia, that moment out of time and space when they touched the divine wisdom before plunging back to temporal consciousness. To understand the individual soul better, we need to have another look at this heaven of heaven.

Here is how Augustine describes it initially in *Confessions* XII.9.9:

> Without doubt the heaven of heaven, which you made in the beginning, is a type of intelligible creature. Although not by any means coeternal with you, O Trinity, it nonetheless participates in your eternity. Because of the sweetness of its joyful contemplation of you, it restrains its mutability. And without any lapse resulting from its having been created, by adhering to you it rises above the whole whirling vicissitude of time.

This heaven is a creature, made by and dependent upon God. It belongs, moreover, to the intelligible level, not the sensible and physical. Its nature is evidently not self-sufficient, since it is described as existing by participation in the eternity of God, its source. As a created and contingent being, it has an inherent tendency towards mutability. Its natural level would appear to be in the temporal realm of change. But it does not move away from God because it exercises contemplation directed back towards God. This reversion upon its source prevents its changing, so that it remains fixed upon its divine creator. Without this unmediated contemplation and participation, it would be lost to the maelstrom of time and change. It is this contemplative fidelity that defines it.

This may sound quite speculative. But Augustine insists that he is, in fact, unspooling what God revealed to him in contemplation, picking up on the language of the divine voice heard without mediation from the Ostian narrative. *Confessions* XII.11.12 explains the contemplative character of this spiritual heaven:

> O blessed one, blessed with you as its everlasting dwelling and source of light! I can find no better name for the Lord's heaven of heaven than your house, which contemplates your delight without any failure or departing to something else. That pure mind in concord is the unity in enduring peace of holy spirits, the citizens of your city in the heaven above this visible heaven.

For the heaven of heaven to cease its contemplation of God, and drift off into mutability would be both disastrous for it and culpable. Augustine makes that quite clear just before this passage in *Confessions* XII.11.11: 'And the motion of the will away from you, who does exist, towards that which exists to a lesser degree, is a fault and a sin.' So the adherence of the heaven of heaven to God is praiseworthy, as it delights in its creator. What is especially striking is that it is neither in time nor is it eternal. It is above the pattern of temporal succession that defines time in the material world. But it is also not eternal, which applies only to God. Instead, it participates in the eternity of God, a state that is dependent upon its continued adherence to God. Thus, it shares with all other creatures the contingency of existence, but its exercise of the love of God prevents its declension into temporal succession. To do otherwise would be culpable, departing from its union of love with God and embracing instead the world of alteration and change.

Note that this decision to adhere to God is a collective one. For the heaven of heaven is a society of individual souls, a congress of blessed spirits, each a citizen of the holy city of heaven. Souls are there joined together in collective contemplation of God. This is, therefore, the true homeland of souls, where their nature as transcendent beings, intended for everlasting – though not eternal – union with God, is fully actualized. It is also a level of reality where their real nature as social beings is exercised by their joint contemplation of their eternal source. They do so as an expression of the freedom invested in them by the creator.

It is not hard to hear those personal narratives of contemplative enlightenment from books VII and IX behind this. This is the level of reality that the souls of Monica and Augustine reached in the vision at Ostia, whose joint character dovetails with the collective society of souls they momentarily joined. But they fell away. We can perhaps understand this better now. The soul is, for Augustine, the culminating expression of the divine creative act, the core of human consciousness and character. It was made to be in union with God. But the fall has somehow separated some souls from God and from each other, distending them into the successiveness of time, and fragmenting their consciousness. Souls can be understood therefore to be individuated spiritually, not by their association with matter and the body. This is a fixed conviction that Augustine will continue to hold even in his late works as he integrated the resurrection body into his understanding of eschatology (*City of God* 22.29). Yet, while individual in nature, souls are meant to contemplate God collectively, forming a society joined by common purpose and mutual volition.

In its earthly life the soul lives an embodied existence in time, yet its goal is to exist in another dimension of reality entirely. This is neither a theory nor a leap of faith for Augustine. He has discovered all this with certainty in the depth of his soul. He insists on that fact in *Confessions* XII, maintaining over and over again that God had revealed all this to him in contemplation. Though beyond words, those insights can be captured through the use of the revealed medium of scripture. To understand our embodied state, we need to use the prism of scripture. That is, in fact, how Augustine frames his famous account of time in *Confessions* XI, as grounded in the Genesis account of creation. As we discussed in Chapter 2, Augustine explains that God exists in the absolute simultaneity of eternity (*Confessions* XI.7.9). Moreover, creation is a spiritual act within the inner life of the Trinity, whereby all things that will emerge into time are ideas within the divine Word. The heaven of heaven is the first created being, neither eternal like God nor fully temporal. In our present life we exist in state whereby our minds are 'distended', stretched out in the temporal sequence of moments that make up time (*Confessions* XI.26.33). We are conscious of past, present and future – full of regrets about the past and full of anxieties about the future. In truth, only the present is real, and that slips instantly out of our consciousness. But past and future are dependent upon the present, because only in the present can our consciousness think about what has gone before and what is yet to come (*Confessions* XI.20.26). Yet because of its instantaneous nature, the present also resembles the simultaneity of eternity. God is perfectly present, but no time can be. Now we live in this distended state, with these three aspects of time before us, and all three are compressed into the consciousness of the present, which lasts but a moment.

Christianity offered Augustine the hope of freeing the soul from the medium of time and reversing its distention. Then the soul would no longer be plagued by all that is temporal, and impermanent, and transitory. This is what soul really means to Augustine, the aspect of human consciousness that can recognize its temporal condition and seek the presence of the eternal. This he describes movingly in *Confessions* XII.16.23:

> I will enter into my chamber and sing songs of love to you, groaning indescribable groans on my pilgrimage and remembering Jerusalem with my heart stretched out towards it, Jerusalem my homeland, Jerusalem my mother; and to you above it, ruler, illuminator, father, tutor, husband, pure and strong delight and solid joy and all ineffably good things, and all these things at once since you are the one supreme and true good. And I will not be turned away until in the peace of this dearest mother, where the first fruits of my spirit are and from which are my certainties, you gather all that I am from this dispersion and deformity and you shape and strengthen me forever, my God, my mercy.

The soul is this aspect of the human person that is capable of transcendence, that which is drawn into the heavenly Jerusalem. Here are the first fruits of the spirit referred to in the vision at Ostia. Here too is the basis of all Augustine's certain knowledge.

Throughout this discussion of the heaven of heaven, Augustine is preoccupied by this theme of human transcendence and the need for divine assistance in achieving it. He keeps his focus on this hope for transcendence, rather than on the soul as an entity as such. He concentrates on describing the self-reflective consciousness found in moral introspection and on demonstrating its transcendence of the body. He is concerned with the interior path to transcendence rather than with taxonomical descriptions of the nature of the soul. As a result, he left a cluster of related questions about the soul unanswered. These cluster around the origin of the soul. The soul is created by God – that is clear. But did it originate in the transcendent realm and then fall into the body after its creation? Or was it created along with the body? Some of the time in his early writings and in the *Confessions*, Augustine seems to have entertained the idea that individual souls might have fallen into the physical world after an earlier, transcendental existence. In *Confessions* I.6.9 he interrogates his infant memories searching for indications of psychic pre-existence. In *Confessions* IV.16.3 he suggests souls should not worry that they might not have any transcendent home to which they can return after their earthly life. That theme of return is recurrent throughout Augustine's early writings and with it the suggestion that souls exist in the world as a form of punishment. *Confessions* XI.9.11 refers to divine Wisdom shining through the clouds that envelop the soul as it falls away into the vicissitudes of time under the weight of its punishments. *Confessions* X.20.29 even suggests two possible theories of pre-existence: an individual loss of the happiness of heaven or a corporate one:

> If knowledge is in the memory, then we once had happiness. I do not ask now whether we were happy singly, or all together in that man who first sinned and in whom we all died and from whom we were all born in misery. I ask only whether the happy life is in the memory.

This is a reference to I Cor. 15.22, construed here to suggest that Adam is symbolic of the community of human souls who turned away from God collectively. Similar accounts of the descent of the soul can be found in Augustine's Platonist source.

However, Augustine never clearly committed himself to any of these options, in part because he was primarily focused on the salvation of the soul (Rombs 2006). He could be surprisingly diffident at times when he is unsure of the evidence. He explains this in a remarkably candid passage in his very late retrospective work, *Reconsiderations*, written just a few years before his death. In this section he is discussing the first work he wrote after his conversion, *Against the Academics*. Here is the first portion of what he said on the subject of the soul's origin (*Reconsiderations* 1.3):

> In another section when I was treating the subject of the soul, I said: 'It will return more safely into heaven.' But I would have been safer if I had said 'will go' rather than 'will return' on account of those who think that human souls either dropped down from heaven or were pushed, and then thrust into bodies

due to their sins. But I did not hesitate to say that because I said 'into heaven' just as I might say 'to God' who is the author and creator. Just as the blessed Cyprian did not hesitate to say: 'For while we possess a body from the earth and a spirit from heaven, we ourselves are both earth and heaven,' and in the Book of Ecclesiastes it is written: 'the spirit will return to God who bestowed it.' This must be understood in this manner so as not to oppose the Apostle who says: 'those not yet born had done neither good nor evil.'

This passage is striking for its continued commitment to the transcendental character of the soul and its independence of the body. Augustine is uncomfortable with penal colony accounts of human life, given his commitment to the creation of the body by God as a good in itself. Any suggestion of a pre-existent life in which ethical decisions were made by the soul is also rejected, citing Rom. 9.11. Nonetheless, he clearly regards the soul as a creature destined for a higher, transcendent station in the structure of reality, which it seeks during its earthly life. Then comes the key claim:

Without question, then, the original region of the happiness of the soul is God himself, who certainly did not beget it from himself, but created it from nothing just as he created the body from the earth. However, what is held about its origins, how it might be in a body, whether it might be from one who was created first when 'man was made a living soul', or similarly whether individual souls are made for individual humans, I did not know then nor do I know now.

That is a clear statement of agnosticism about the soul's proximate origins. But it is also a categorical statement that the ultimate origin of the soul is God the creator.

It puts strong emphasis on the transcendent nature of the soul and underscores that the real issue for Augustine is the soul's heavenly destiny. That lies with God. This is a theme that goes back to his earliest writing. *On the Greatness of the Soul* I.2 reads: 'I believe that God himself, who created the soul, is in a certain sense its own residence and home.' Thus, language of return to God might be countenanced if it means the soul's reunion with its creator and source, rather than its recovering a life before embodiment but since left behind. Read this way, the great descriptions of the longing of the soul for transcendence are psalms of lament for its fallen state and for the union with its true author. That aching desire for the eternal is what defines human existence for Augustine. What he calls the soul is the locus of that longing for everlasting union. This is, for Augustine, the abiding goal of human existence, to be freed from the deformity of the fall and to be united with the eternal Father.

# 4

# Evil

*But wanting to discover the causes of these defects is like
wanting to see darkness or hear silence.*

To know God is to know evil. That was what Augustine discovered
through his experience of contemplation in Milan. Those moments
of enlightenment etched in sharp relief his own soul's separation
from God and his complicity in its fallen state. Contemplation of
transcendent Wisdom led him to realize that the soul alone is the
root cause of evil and the human condition. 'Augustine would insist
that ours is a self-made darkness, that the heart's darkness is our
own doing ... [and] that darkness came to occupy and unmake the
very core of our being' (Harmless, 2014, 5). In this chapter we will
endeavour to sort out what Augustine meant by this startling claim
and to discern how it formed the foundation of his approach to evil. To
do so we will need to be alert once again to how different Augustine's
reflections are from contemporary philosophy and theology and
their treatments of 'the problem of evil'. That is because Augustine
approached the matter with a purpose distinct from philosophy and
theology as understood today. So for us to understand Augustine,
we'll need to examine our own conventions of thought before we can
try to capture Augustine's insights on this compelling matter.

## Contemporary Theodicy

It would difficult to live in this world and not be appalled by the
dark reality of evil. Both physical and moral evil seem to demand

some explanation, some reason, for their existence. Absent such an account, the world seems meaningless and an affront to our innate expectation of rationality. But any such intellectual response would inevitably be drawn into giving an account of goodness as well, for good and evil are inextricably linked. In the grim societies of antiquity, when humans survived against mortality rates substantially higher than today and war was a seasonal occupation, the power of evil was manifest everywhere. And so we can find a variety of approaches to evil in the philosophies of antiquity, among which were those that sought to ground both good and evil in a single first principle. In some ways these ancient monotheisms – Pagan, Jewish and Christian – faced a more difficult task than other approaches. Both pagan polytheism and ancient dualism attributed good and evil to multiple, often conflicting, forces. Moreover, they regarded evil as an unavoidable fact of the nature of things. As we discovered in our analysis of Manichaeism in Chapter 1, evil was not so much something to be explained as something that just existed as an elemental aspect of reality. It was, therefore, simply a primordial force to be dealt with.

But the apparent plausibility of those accounts was belied by surface quality of their explanations. It is apparent that by late antiquity attributing good and evil to multiple powers had come to seem increasingly inadequate. It invited a further demand for ultimacy, some explanation of where these conflicting divinities or powers themselves came from. Beyond that conceptual drive, we can also discern that the great religious philosophies of late antiquity were keen to offer their adherents a spiritual path beyond evil, a way for the human soul to find a deeper resolution to the evils encountered in life and a means to secure a permanent hold on the good. As we have discussed already, these ancient philosophies joined theory and practice intimately. To understand them requires continuing recognition of that connection. But it also means that much of what we find in the ancient texts is different in character from contemporary discussions of God and evil. Back then the emphasis was on finding the right path for the soul in its journey beyond the travails of this life and into future one, whereas now the focus is on finding a theory that makes the existence of God conceptually compatible with the fact of evil.

If we wish to understand recent discussion of God and evil, a good place to look is the most influential contemporary book on evil and Augustine: John Hick's *Evil and the God of Love* (Hick 1966). Hick's book helped to set the terms of debate in what is commonly called 'theodicy'. Theodicy may be defined as 'the defense of the justice and righteousness of God in the face of the fact of evil' (Hick 1966, 6). As thus represented, theodicy is a product of the Enlightenment and its lineage goes back to the philosopher Leibniz, who published a book by that title in 1710. Modern theodicy centres on the questions of whether the reality of evil leads to the denial of the existence of God. On moral grounds the existence of evil often seems like compelling counter-evidence to the existence of God. As such, debates in theodicy are intellectual disputes about God, conceptual in character and distinct from any subjective appropriation of God. Theodicy is, therefore, an exercise of critical theory.

In his study, Hick is keen to establish that wall of separation between theory and practice. He insists that the proper task of theodicy is rational and objective analysis, unimpeded by the difficulties involved in coping with evil. This sharp distinction is foundational to the field, and integral to securing its place within academic philosophy of religion, in contrast to applied or pastoral theology. Hick regards Augustine not only as a theodicist in this modern sense but also as the fountainhead of Western Christian theodicy. As such he assimilates Augustine to the modern project of theodicy and in particular to its assumed context of theoretical debate about divine existence. He does so by reconstructing Augustine's thought, drawing together themes from different works into a larger theoretical construct. The chief components of his recovered model of Augustinian theodicy include, first, the free-will defence that evil is a product of the free choice of creatures; second, the claim that evil is the lack of goodness or being; third, the principle of plenitude – that no possibility of divine production can remain unactualized; and fourth, the aesthetic theme – that evil contributes to the perfection of the universe when seen as a whole.

Hick considers these elements as theoretical assertions by Augustine intended to mitigate claims that the existence of evil undermines the plausibility the God's existence. But once reconstructed in this fashion, Hick goes on to insist that Augustine's theodicy is unsatisfactory. He maintains that the free-will defence fails because Augustine has no way to explain rationally the initial choice of evil. Moreover, Hick regards the other three pillars of

Augustinian theodicy – the non-being of evil, the principle of plenitude and the aesthetic theme, as relics of pagan Platonism. Augustinian theodicy is, therefore, both incoherent and inconsistent with Christian theism.

Hick's representation of Augustinian theodicy bears repeating today both because of its influence in framing subsequent readings of Augustine and because it is emblematic of the problems associated with the project of theodicy itself. An initial difficulty is rooted in the nature of Hick's reading of Augustine. In order for Augustine to be plausibly treated as the fountainhead of Western Christian theodicy, Hick had to assemble themes in his thought into an apparently coherent theoretic construct, an 'amalgamated theodicy' – to use Terry Tilley's phrase (Tilley 1991, 131–2). Its elements were extracted from different works written to differing purposes from distinct stages in Augustine's development. Hick homogenizes early works like the anti-Manichaean *On the Nature of the Good* side by side with middle period works like *Confessions* and late works like *City of God*. Moreover, ideas in Augustine that are at best secondary – like the principle of plenitude or the aesthetic theme – become major theoretical planks in Hick's reconstruction. Yet reading Augustine in this fashion rests on the tacit assumption that his goal was to hammer together a systematic theology. But, on the contrary, *Reconsiderations*, his great theological retrospective, makes amply clear that he worked on various issues and controversies over his long career, often shifting and adjusting his views. In a sense, Hick became Augustine's theological editor, revising, collecting and accentuating ideas from different contexts in order to derive a theoretical solution to the problem of evil, a theodicy in the modern sense.

That assumption is crucial to the interpretive trajectory in contemporary philosophy of religion initiated by Hick: the supposition that Augustine was doing theodicy in a fashion that can be straightforwardly assimilated into modern debates in that field. But a deeper problem of commensurability emerges from this modern reading of Augustine as a theodicist, for the very project of theodicy involves assumptions that Augustine did not share. We need to reflect on two of the most salient of these in the interest of moving beyond them.

First, theodicy rests on the fundamental assumption that theoretical answers to the existence of evil are determined by a rational observer who seeks a coherent account of divine purpose. Theodicy thus relies on discursive knowledge of the divine nature, such that the justice of God can be lucidly understood in the face of evil. Some degree of cognitive surety about divine causality and its purpose is necessary, therefore, to warrant the claims of the theodicist. At its core, theodicy seeks a rational, objective, theoretical account of God.

Second, it follows that theodicy is conducted by a disinterested philosopher, engaged in problem-solving. Hick is especially keen to press this point. Theodicy must be sharply separated from actually dealing with evil or from the emotions attendant upon that struggle. Indeed, it might be said that theodicy is best described by a solitary, armchair discipline, conducted by the atomized self. As Kenneth Surin has observed, theodicy rests on a sort of 'cognitional individualism' (Surin 1986, 20). It is the individual judgement of the theodicist that determines – for example – whether a version of the free-will defence seems intuitively plausible or not.

Neither of these interpretive assumptions is commensurable with the thought of Augustine. As we have discovered, Augustine is not primarily interested in distanced knowledge of God. That is because he has only limited confidence in the powers of the discursive intellect, whose results are at best flawed and provisional. Cognitive judgement is an act that involves the will, in particular the dispositions of the knowing subject. And, for Augustine, these are conditioned by the moral character of the self. As a result, the apparently disinterested judgements of the rational philosopher are covertly acts of self-expression. Augustine regards those judgements as the products of human cognitive incapacitation, rooted in moral flaws of our own making. Thus, theodicy is subtly infected with aspects of the evil it purports to explain. Moreover, the project of disinterested reflection is itself a conceit grounded in cognitive pride, in the sinister self-nescience that Augustine sometimes associated with pagan philosophy. Without conversion of the soul, without the illumination of grace, theodicy is fatally flawed. The project of theoretical appraisal of God is thus of limited value because true knowledge of God involves transforming the soul so that it might move beyond observation into communion.

It might be said, then, that Augustine did not have a free-will defence of the goodness of God in the face of evil, nor indeed any theodicy at all. The modern search for an Augustinian theodicy is a dead end, for the project of theodicy was never Augustine's own. And yet, having said all this it is important to recognize that, while the modern notion of theodicy fails to capture Augustine's thinking on the problem of evil, he did indeed see evil as an affront to moral rationality, something that required intellectual framing. So, while theodicy may be an inadequate description of Augustine's efforts to address evil, it points towards the need for a more capacious understanding of Augustine's thinking on the matter. To its recovery we now turn.

# Confessing Evil

Augustine's approach to evil centres on two fundamental insights: the non-being of evil and the irrationality of evil. As we discovered already, both insights emerged from his conversionary experience of contemplation in Milan. They are thus part of that larger understanding of transcendent reality that had flooded his consciousness. Any serious effort to understand Augustine on evil must begin there. We need to reconsider both of these often misunderstood ideas by tracing their foundations in the thought of Augustine. This representation of evil is one of the most passionately described features of Augustine's conversion narrative in *Confessions* VII. And that is so because Augustine claims repeatedly that he came to discern the source and character of evil in the very same instance of transformative insight in which the nature of God was disclosed to him. Such a claim is, of course, a challenge to a host of modern conventions and invites our scrutiny.

As just noted, Augustine was accustomed to regard metaphysics or theology not as abstract theory about the divine but as a map sketching the soul's spiritual path. The goal was not theoretical appraisal but spiritual communion. Augustine insisted that his life was changed by seeking for transcendence and then coming to discover powerfully, and directly, and experientially, his soul's reality in God. Out of that insight tumbled a new way to understand evil. That was not a theory, but the articulation of a cognitive experience so deeply known within the innermost recesses of the soul that it went beyond the categories of everyday experience or thought. And that is where Augustine's grasp of evil is to be found.

As we have seen in Chapter 2, Augustine states that he had several experiences of divine transcendence, both before and after his conversion. He is quite insistent about this and he discusses what he discovered both in his early writings and in *Confessions*. We see this in *On the Greatness of the Soul*, written in Rome around 387/8 just after the events of his conversion and thus his earliest treatment of the subject. There he iterates a seven-stage account of the soul's interior path to transcendence, at once a prescriptive template and an early record of ascension. Most importantly, he emphasizes that the soul, even at the penultimate stage of interior ascension when it has begun to achieve an inner grasp of truth, is nonetheless prone to recidivism. This failure at transcendence is vividly attributed to the moral opacity of the fallen soul (*On the Greatness of the Soul* 33.75):

> Anyone who wants to do so before they have been cleansed and healed is so repelled by the light of truth that they think there is not only nothing good in it but even much evil. And they reject the name of truth from it, and with some desire and miserable pleasure, they flee back into their own darkness where they are able to endure their sickness and curse its cure.

But those souls who persevere arrive 'at the vision and contemplation of truth', a dwelling place for the enjoyment of the perfect, true and eternal good. This we are told is what great souls saw and see. Notice that this account of interior ascension bears the character mentioned above. It is not theory, but an attestation of practice.

The larger implications of this graded ascension into higher levels of reality are surveyed in another early work, *On True Religion*, written after his return home to Thagaste around 389/90. There Augustine begins by praising Platonism for its commitment to an ultimate, transcendent God who is superior to our minds. From it he tells us that he has come to realize fully that transcendent truth can be sought only with the mind and not with the senses, but only if the mind has been cured (*On True Religion* iii.3). Then the enjoyment of eternal contemplation is given to the rational soul and through it comes eternal life. Here, Augustine begins to work out the implications of this transcendentalism for the understanding of evil. He concentrates on the opacity of the soul that frustrated the soul's ascension initially in the account we just considered in *On the*

*Greatness of the Soul.* That failure lay in the soul's perplexing inner choice to fall away from God even as it came into the divine presence. In *On True Religion* he comes to recognize that the core of evil lies in the soul's own movement away from God, a choice rooted in a misplaced sense of the self. And that misdirects the soul away from reality itself towards what is less real. The choice of that vector constitutes evil (*On True Religion* ix.22). Augustine is now clear that the recognition of God's transcendent goodness has disclosed the reality of the soul's choice to separate itself from God. He summarizes the movement of the soul away from its source and then back to it again as follows (*On True Religion* lv.113):

> ... one God from whom we exist, through whom we exist, in whom we exist; from whom we departed, to whom we have been made dissimilar, by whom we have not been permitted to perish. The principle to whom we are hastening, the beauty we seek, and the grace through which we are reconciled.

The initial choice to withdraw away from God is the primordial source of evil and the disfigurement of the image of God within us. This can only be reversed by divine grace. Thus, to come to know God is to come to know the enormity of the soul's self-destructive loss.

These early texts are tautly written, with theory, contemplative method and personal attestation interwoven. *Confessions* is the ultimate expression of these same elements. Here we find the root of evil sharply exposed by the soul's exercise of contemplation. But Augustine's recognition of evil as the privation of the Good is not articulated as a philosophical theory. It is, instead, a recognition that falls out from Augustine's interior experience of transcendence. It is the cognitive fruit of contemplation.

Augustine's arresting notion of evil as insubstantial and parasitic on the reality of God can be found articulated just after the first ascension narrative of *Confessions* VII.10.16, which we examined in Chapter 1. There we find the immediate knowledge of transcendent Wisdom joined to the painful recognition of the soul's fallen condition. We might recall that the narrative begins with the soul turning into its inner depths through divine assistance and discovering a higher level of reality. Raised up by divine love, the soul discerns eternal being itself and simultaneously realizes that it is not yet being. Repelled by the light of divine being and shuddering with love and awe, the soul recognizes that it exists in a state of dissimilarity from eternal being. In its unmediated recognition of God as true love, eternal truth and beloved eternity, the soul also has immediate recognition of its fallen state. While God is perfect being, the soul is not. It is not capable of sustaining the unmediated association with God that had been granted to it. The perfect being of God overwhelms the soul, confronting it with its state of separation from God. Thus, to know God is also to know the self as culpably fallen. Those two searing truths are inescapably conjoined.

From this moment of transcendence several further insights then emerge in *Confessions* VII.11.17-19. First, the things that are below God are discovered to have only relative existence. They neither absolutely exist – like God – nor do they entirely lack being. They exist because they come from God, but they are not wholly or autonomously real, since they are not God. This is presented as an immediate, reflective outcome of the first experience of transcendence. Here is how Augustine explains this:

> And I examined the other things below you, and I saw that they are neither entirely being nor entirely not being. They have a certain being because they are from you, but they are not being because they are not what you are. What truly is that which remains without change.

Augustine says that he recognized as well the goodness of all things, even of the contingent beings of the created world, despite their being prone to change and destruction. Their very existence is a good in itself, and as long as they exist, they are good. They are good because they came forth into the contingency of existence from the eternal creator.

That then opens up a new grasp of evil. Augustine says in *Confessions* VII.12.18 that whatever things exist are good. That then means that evil – about whose origins he had been puzzling – is not a substance, for if it were a substance, it then would be good. And so evil has no being, that is, it has no independent existence. It is not in itself a substance; it has no hold on existence on its own. But it is, instead, an epiphenomenon of divine creation, something that depends on created things. Moreover, he has made the following discovery: 'For you, evil doesn't exist at all; and not only for you but for your created universe' (*Confessions* VII.13.9). We need to ponder this arresting claim, for it is one of the central insights of his conversionary experience. First, how is it that evil does not exist for God? And second, how does it not exist for the created universe? The answers to these questions rest upon Augustine's contemplative recognition that God is infinite being itself. God is really real, the only true reality. As infinite being, God might be thought of as the force field of existence, the infinite web of existence within which all finite beings exist and upon which they are existentially dependent. This is what creation means, the self-expression in finite reality of the infinite Good. And that creation is itself good, though made up of finite beings. What God made is good, and evil has no reality within that creative self-articulation. Here is Augustine's account of this (*Confessions* VII.15.21):

> I considered other things, and I saw that to you they owe their being, and that all things are defined by you, not spatially, but because you hold them in your hand, which is truth. And all things are true to the extent that they have being; nor is anything false unless it thought to be when it does not. But I realized this because things fit not just in their own places but in addition in their own times. I saw too that you, who alone are eternal, did not begin to work after innumerable periods of time, since all periods of time, both those that have passed and those that will pass, neither pass away nor come to be except through you bringing that about and also abiding.

Evil has no part in God's creation, and it has – in that sense – no reality for God. To put this another way: evil is the vector of away from God, so that for God, evil has no being at all. How this vector comes about we'll need to consider in the next section. But first we need to unpack further this vision of the perfection of creation. It rests on Augustine's contemplation of divine transcendence, his recognition that God is eternal and therefore outside time, so that the succession of time emerges out of eternity and into creation. The moments of past and future are bound by the finite being of creation and are expressions of infinite being itself. Moreover, the elements of creation, as expressions of the Good, are themselves good and they form patterns that are harmonious. This is where the aesthetic theme, identified by Hick, it comes to the fore, not as a theoretical claim but rather as the contemplative recognition of the rational order of creation.

Augustine explains this in personal terms (*Confessions* VII.13.19–14.20). He admits that as a Manichee he had accepted that good and evil were two conflicting energies within the spatio-temporal cosmos. He had thought evil as breaking into the order of the world as a malevolent power. But that thinking was wrongheaded in numerous ways. It assumed that evil was a substance in its own right, one that was powerful and active. In addition, it had led him to identify many elements of the world as instances of evil. But finite things may appear so when taken in isolation or when the conflicts that develop with the confines of space and time are emphasized. Yet, all these elements of creation fit into larger patterns of congruity and order when taken together. It is only when he woke up to the realization that God is both infinite and transcendent that he was able to see the insubstantiality of evil. God is the transcendent Good and there is, as it were, no way to get outside that infinite reality.

Once he perceived that within the depths of his soul, there was no turning back. Augustine insists that these insights emerged from contemplation. He saw these truths intellectually and they were made clear to him immediately. He did not infer them from experience; neither did he interpret the characteristics of the experience to yield those conclusions. Instead, he says that he discerned these things clearly and indubitably. Augustine's account of non-being of evil is not, therefore, an abstract theory, but something that he regards as disclosed in the moment of interior contemplation and beyond doubt. It became the bedrock of his lifelong commitment to monotheism.

With this representation of evil as the privation of goodness and being, comes the recognition of its irrational origins in the will. That understanding too is knit into his contemplative recognition of divine transcendence. In *Confessions* VII.16.22 Augustine says once again that his inquiry into the nature of iniquity led him not to a substance but to the perversity of the will. The soul exercised its freedom to focus on itself and twist away from the highest reality, the Good. In so doing, it abandoned its true life in communion with God and swelled with what is external to it. As noted in Chapter 3, this is an act of perverse self-abandonment for Augustine, a loss of the intimate for the external. The soul seeks a false individuation, a diminished existence fraught with contingency. Thus, we see stitched together here the two main themes of Augustine's account of evil, non-being and irrationality, both direct insights from contemplation. This initial account of contemplation helps us, therefore, to understand the character of Augustine's claims about evil. To clarify this further, we need to be reminded of the second descriptions of interior ascension from *Confessions* VII.17.23. There the soul ascended to a more perfect level of existence, to the true and complete reality of God. In doing so it left behind what is less real and less perfect. The narrative begins by describing the limitations of contemplation for the fallen soul, much like we saw in *On the Greatness of the Soul*. As the contemplative soul goes deeper into itself, it moves beyond the power of discursive reasoning into an unmediated intellectual perception of that which is real and unchanging. And then its moral status brings it crashing back to the surface of temporal consciousness. The weight of its immoral state prevents its continued enjoyment of eternity, for the soul cannot escape the material level on which it is morally centred. The soul is restricted in its ability to associate with God because of its own self-constructed moral identity.

This false individuation of the soul has a social dimension as well. And so evil does as well. Early on in *Confessions* II, in a famous scene, Augustine recounts how his adolescent gang – the Wreckers – had stolen some pears in a nocturnal raid. He had no need for the fruit; indeed, he had better fruit at home. Subtly reprising the garden scene in Eden, Augustine admits there was no reason for this act. He did it on an irrational impulse rooted in his heart. This is what he says (*Confessions* II.4.9):

> Behold my heart, Lord, behold my heart, which at the bottom of the abyss you pitied. Now behold my heart as it tells you what it sought there when I was evil for no reason and had no motive for my wickedness except wickedness itself. It was foul and I loved it. I loved being ruined. I loved my rebellion, not that for which I rebelled but my rebellion itself. And my shameful soul leaped from your firmament to utter destruction. I desired shame not for some end, but shame itself.

What he did, he did out of perversity, out of self-assertion, out of an urge for self-destruction. All that points directly to his central claim: that evil is irrational in itself.

But he was also alert to the fact that would never have attempted this pear heist without his gang. He says that he would never have done it alone. He did it because he loved being part of the group. So his pleasure was not in the pears but in a crime committed in association with his friends. And they did it because it was not allowed, echoing the disobedience of Adam and Eve. He sums up the larger meaning of this outwardly insignificant transgression in sweeping theological terms (*Confessions* II.6.14):

> Thus the soul fornicates when it turns away from you. It seeks but does not find outside you the things that are pure and clear, unless it returns to you. All imitate you perversely, causing themselves to be far from you and exalting themselves over against you. But thus by imitating you they reveal that you are the creator of all nature and that there is no place to slip away completely from you. Therefore what was it that I loved in that theft, and in what way did I imitate my lord viciously and perversely?

It is noteworthy that Augustine employs the spatial imagery of turning away from the Good and searching outside God for satisfaction. In the theft, he was seeking pleasure in an illicit act for no reason other than it was not permitted. That perversity of will is exemplary of human evil. Evil is thus a senseless distancing of the soul from the Good and an exaltation of the self. It is the choice of a lesser self, a self emptied of its native goodness and thus of its inherent being. As Augustine's discourse of distance reminds us, this is a decline of the soul from its proximity to true being and an embrace of a diminished level of being. In its assertive choice of a lesser good, the soul has chosen to degrade its very self.

## Scattered Traces of His Being

'To myself I was death.' This is a hard truth, that each of us contributes to the existence of evil. We sustain it by the choices we make; otherwise, it would have no reality. To blame God for evil is to miss the point, and culpably so. For to do so is to rage against the only real Good, and to obscure from ourselves the bitter truth of our own choices. We deny our complicity in evil and look to blame others, above all, God. This too is an expression of the self-regard that was the root of evil in the first place. Yet, even in our moral poverty, the diminished self stills searches restlessly for the Good. Augustine discovered this both in those moments of contemplative enlightenment that reoriented his understanding, and in the continuing revelation of the divine through scripture. These revealed mysteries are the antidote to the mystery of our complicity in the fall, offering the soul medicinal and restorative power, leading the soul to renewed communion with God. Meditation on the divine word through scripture is thus regarded by Augustine as a habitual, if preliminary, mode of contemplating God.

This is where we can best come to understand Augustine on evil. Late in the *Confessions* XII.27.37–28.38, Augustine makes a revealing distinction about reading scripture. He contrasts two types of Catholic readers: The first are those who read scripture literally, while the second read with an eye towards the rich fruit of wisdom hidden behind the text. Readers of the first type think of God as if he were a human being, or a power located in some remote place who suddenly decided to make heaven and earth. They assume that God actually said, 'let there be light', and as soon as the sound of those words ceased to resonate, the world came into existence. Their thinking is thus crudely anthropomorphic and deeply conditioned by space and time, by 'a bodily way of imagining'. He says that those in first group are like infants in their faith or birds not yet ready to fly the nest. He concedes that they may get the basic point of God's creation correctly, but they are as yet not ready to go further. But the second group are. They can ascend through the images of scripture to a transcendental understanding of God, and recover a unity with the divine One. Here is the full text of this illuminating passage from *Confessions* XII.28.38:

> When they read or hear these words, O God, they see that all past and future times are surpassed by your eternal and stable permanence, and yet there is no temporal creature that you did not make. Your will, since it is what you are, is not in any way changed, nor has it become what it was not at an earlier time; and it is through your will that you made all things. You did not create out of yourself in your own likeness, which is the form of all things, but out of nothing, a formless dissimilarity that is formed by your likeness. And it returns to you, the One, according to its ordained capacity, given to each thing based on

its own genus. And so all were made very good whether they remain close to you or, according to their degree of distance in time or space, in beautiful variations which they either cause or undergo. These things see and rejoice in the light of your truth to whatever small extent each is able.

There is no evil in this account of creation. If we pull on the strands of this text we can grasp why. Augustine is once again drawing out the ramifications of his enlightenment experiences. He begins with God's transcendence – that is what the literal, materialist reader cannot discern. Augustine can concede that God might be said to exercise volition in creating, but that decision is not a sudden choice in time by a God existing in the physical universe. God's will is identical with God's nature, which we know is best thought of as love, goodness and eternity. The decision to create should be understood to be rooted in the timeless goodness of God and an expression of infinite love. It is the unfolding of the eternal into time. Yet, God did not unspool his own reality into the world he created. Creation was made from nothing in the likeness of God, but not from the divine nature itself. And created things should thus be recognized as all good and prone by their created natures to seek return to the One from whence they emerged into time and space. This great vision of an eternal God creating the great chain of temporal being is what contemplative readers of Genesis can discover behind the literal text. They can thereby come to grasp the truth about God's creation now in this life and, more importantly, use this insight to further the return of their souls to God. Scriptural contemplation of the account of creation is therefore anagogical for Augustine; it promotes the soul's turn back to God. In doing so the human soul can join the general pattern of the created order, all of whose creatures desire – in varying degrees – to unite with their divine source.

Evil is not part of this picture. Augustine had discerned in those initial acts of contemplation that God is infinite goodness, and his soul's ascensions to God had proceeded through increased levels of perfection. Moreover, evil had been exposed as the absence or loss of the good, not an independent entity produced by God. For that reason it was immediately evident that evil was never anything that God could create. So what is good came into existence by God's act of creative expression, but evil had no divine origin and was never part of that primordial translation of eternity into time. For this reason Augustine regards the cosmos as fundamentally good. He insists on this, based in part on the Genesis narrative, and rules out the notion that the physical world is flawed. This cosmos emerged into time out of divine perfection and God saw that it was good.

But what about natural catastrophes or human diseases? How are they accounted for? To understand Augustine's approach to that ever-present question, we need to be alert to the mode of his response. This is where the project of theoretical theodicy misreads Augustine. In his vast late work *The City of God*, written after the fall of Rome in 410, Augustine confronted this issue clearly (*Confessions* XII.4). There he distinguishes between natural and moral evil, but regards only the latter to be evil in the strict sense. The physical world is full of natural evils. These are indeed evils, he admits, from our limited perspective, and God as creator is responsible for them. But Augustine does not present his readers with a theodicy in response. Instead, he counsels acceptance of the natural ills found in our material world in view of the certainty of God's goodness. The physical world has complex ecological patterns amid continual change, as things are born and flourish and decay. We may sometimes derive little delight in that grand cosmic order, partly because we have difficulty observing the macrocosm from our restricted vantage point, but more so because we suffer physical pain as a result of our mortal nature. As he says: 'And so it is the nature of a thing, considered in itself, and not according to our advantage or disadvantage, that gives glory to its maker.' But in offering such observations, Augustine does construct a theory to explain the ways of God and solve the problem of natural evil. He is not arguing an 'aesthetic theodicy', as Hick would have it, in which the beauty of the whole mosaic of creation would justify specific instances of natural evil. Instead, he is directing the Christian soul towards a deepening relationship with God whose ways are beyond reckoning. With respect to natural evil he recommends the following (*City of God* XII.4):

> So for us, when we have contemplated order in less suitable things, it is right to believe in the providence of the creator, and we must not venture to blame the work of such a maker in any respect through the temerity of human vanity.

It is the goodness of God – in which the soul participates and to which it is returning – that needs to be our focus.

The great danger, then, is the immature approach to God that Augustine repeatedly states is inadequate. That includes both literalist readings of scripture and, more generally, efforts to theorize about God. These modes of reflection about God are flawed for several reasons. They rely on a finite conception of God that is either anthropomorphic or at least dependent upon the conditions that exist in the physical cosmos. And so such discourse rests on a subtle materialism that underlies its efforts. For the literalist reader, that means describing God in human terms, as a power who decides in time to create the world or who exercises his all-powerful volition to unleash tsunamis against those who annoy him. For the theorist, including even the sophisticated thinker who grasps God's transcendence, it means presuming to understand the purposes of an infinite God according to finite conceptual models. Thus, to regard God as a perfect agent is to reify God, reducing the infinite to a finite perfection. Worse yet, such efforts distance the soul from the Good, in which it lives and has its being. Theoretical justifications of God in the face of natural evil thus compound the soul's estrangement. Theodicy is at best misguided, an exercise in seeing reality through the categories of the material world with which the embodied is comfortable. At worst, it is the expression of the soul's culpable insistence on construing reality according to its own self-interest.

That brings us back to moral evil and the epicentre of Augustine's account of evil: the non-being of evil and the irrationality of its origins. Augustine regards moral wickedness as evil in the truest sense, for while natural evil is part of God's creation, moral evil is the result of choice that marred it. Moral evil is a perversion, a vitiation of the good, a culpable flaw. While the good may exist on its own, evil cannot (*City of God* XII.3). It is parasitic on the existing good which it corrupts. It is thus contrary to the good as well as a mute witness to the existence of the goodness which it defaced. It had its source in the irrational choice of Adam and Eve, and before that in the rebellion of angels – something that Augustine treats in *The City of God* at some length (XI). It must be admitted, however, that the exact quotient between moral and natural evil is unknown. This is due to the subtle pervasiveness of moral evil, which forms a vast tapestry of social evil throughout human society and culture. Even apparent natural evils are often instances of moral evil in disguise. The principal example is death. While seemingly a biological condition for mammals, in the case of humans it came into existence through the sin of Adam and Eve. But more mundane events that seem to be accidents can have their roots in moral failures, for example, in human failures of attention. Moreover, systemic evils like malnutrition or poverty might be traced to social structures or cultural norms. The list is lengthy. But beneath all these evils are decision whose dimensions are ethical and whose sources are thus to be found in human wickedness and moral failure.

The depravity of human evil has, therefore, exercised a false creation, generating a social and cultural web so ubiquitous that is often taken as a natural condition. We can hardly begin to encompass it in our minds or find a vantage point to survey it. Worse still, in the case of moral evil, we resist even doing so. Partly our perceptions of society and culture are torqued by our own self-oriented disposition, for while we may not be wholly wicked, we are lazy-minded and prone to take things as they are. Worst still, we resist self-reflection and fear exposing our complicity in evil.

Yet, it is not all theological gloom and doom for Augustine. Evil in all its forms can conduce the soul over its lifetime to engage in the introspective contemplation that he modelled in the *Confessions*. Introspective contemplation offers a chance to redress the fall in this life, restoring the soul's association with its divine source through grace. And in doing so, Augustine believes that the soul reverses the vector away from God that constitutes evil. Through interior contemplation the soul achieves transcendence not just of the diminished reality of space-time, but also of the false individuation that it chose when pursuing an existence distanced from God. So Augustine's account proposes that moral evil can be overcome not just after death but, at least, fractionally now in life. The redress of evil is revealed to souls who trust in God and seek communion with him. To those souls the overcoming of evil is revealed even now by the Christ, the divine Wisdom. That means that Augustine's efforts to sketch some framework for the soul to see a larger divine purpose in evil must be nested in his view that Christian souls are even in this life cultivating transcendence. They live 'in Christ'. So our hope lies outside the tapestry of moral evil, in the only true reality of God. That God of love revealed himself in space and time, and his Christ broke the bonds of moral evil and death, shattering the moral landslip of this fallen world. It is he who offers to return us to ourselves and to him. Here is Augustine's great summary of that vision from *City of God* XI.28:

> Therefore we are now human beings created in the image of our creator, whose eternity is true, whose truth is eternal, whose love is eternal and true, who himself is a trinity of eternity, truth and love, without confusion and separation. Those things that are inferior to us because they could not exist at all by themselves, could not maintain any sort of appearance, nor keep or seek any sort of structure, unless they had been created by him who supremely exists and is supremely wise and supremely good. Running, as it were, over all the things which he made in such marvelous stability, we might collect his scattered traces sometimes more clearly, sometimes less so. And gazing at his image in ourselves, and returning to ourselves, let us rise up like the younger son in the gospel story and let us go back to him from whom we have withdrawn by our sin. There our being will have no death, there our knowledge will have no error and our love will have no impediment.

Augustine's account of evil emerges, therefore, from the epistemic character of his accounts of transcendence. As we have seen repeatedly, in contemplation the soul enters a zone of reality that cannot be captured by the discourse of sense perception and the concepts of empirical consciousness. So what Augustine cannot do is capture discursively the reality of transcendent wisdom. Nor can it be articulated theoretically. Discursive reasoning is superseded in contemplation, but so too is theodicy. For what the soul discovers in contemplation is the false reality that its choice of evil had initiated. That recognition is not theory, but an insight that obviates the distanced, theoretical claims of theodicy. Moreover, it is now clear why rational theodicy fails to capture the nature of evil. For the soul's choice of declension away from God resists conceptualization precisely because it is an option towards what lacks conceptual shape. It is the soul's inchoate embrace of a lesser self for which no account can be rendered. To construct an Augustinian theodicy is, therefore, to miss his insights into both the nature of God and evil. As Augustine put it: seeking a rational account of the causes of evil and the fall is 'like wishing to see darkness or hear silence' (*City of God* XII.7). No theodicy can theoretically explain the enormity of that irrational act. For evil has its origins in the self-made darkness of the human heart.

# 5

# The Rise of Christianity

*God became human so that humans could become divine.*

That catchy slogan was the rallying cry of Catholic Christianity in late antiquity. It captured the imagination of Augustine and became the cornerstone of his theology after his conversion in 386. To many Christians today it may sound like a heresy. That suggests – as we move to conclude this book on Augustine – that we might need to step back and think about what made Catholic Christianity so compelling to Augustine, and what separates us from his thought. We might reflect on the salience of Catholic Christianity, what made it rise above the many other religions and philosophies that Augustine encountered. Augustine offers us an especially good vantage point to consider this matter since we can see both the shape of the Christianity he adopted and the points about it that clearly appealed to him. And so he offers us an opening to reconsider – ancient Christianity.

## Deification

The religions of late antiquity made human salvation their core. Religions, after all, address central issues in human life. For the world of late antiquity – as the idea of the worth of individuals was gaining ground – that dominant question was the fate of human beings after death (Taylor 1989, Sorabji 2006, Siedentop 2014). Augustine was no exception in his relentless desire to be rescued from oblivion, and his religious trajectory describes an arc across the range of ancient options. On one end of the spectrum of beliefs on human survival of death were those that regarded immortality as a natural property of the soul. Augustine gave two of these a try – each a very different option. As we saw, Augustine was a committed Manichee for many years. That meant that he believed that his deepest self was a divine spirit, a spark of the Good. It was indefectible and immutable, though it could be captured and immured by the evil power of matter. Although a materialist account, it was a strong position to hold, for the spirit was, by nature, divine. After he dropped out of Manichaeism, Augustine's next stop was Platonism, if not as a member then at least as a serious reader. Here he discovered what was the strongest ancient account of psychic immortality. Platonists regarded the soul as immaterial and destined to repeated incarnations – until it could deepen its participation in the transcendent world of being, and be freed from returning to a body. Its earthly consciousness and memories may not survive this process of repeated incarnation, but it did retain its personal moral character, which was being educated throughout this process. The goal was achieving such a stable relation to the eternal level of being and goodness that the soul would no longer desire to descend into the physical world. The Good maintained a deeper magnetism that drew the soul towards itself, though it did not exercise personal attention or assistance. Nor did the Good change the nature of the soul, only ennoble it. Nonetheless, this was also a robust account of the soul, specifying immortality as the native destiny of the human soul.

Augustine might well have bought into that theory, but instead he says it only led him to discover the God of Catholic Christianity. This God he believed was present within his soul and brought him into momentary union through a personal moment of enlightenment. His soul was shown to be created immortal but insufficient in power to achieve its own release from the powers of evil and death. The *Confessions* is the autobiographical verification of that point. And so for Augustine, immortality was as much a problem as a solution, opening the soul to the need for rescue from on high. From the standpoint of antiquity, Augustine's Christianity regarded the soul to be shallow, fallen and deeply flawed, with but one earthly life to lead. Yet, Augustine's portrait of the impoverishment of the soul also pointed to the magnificence of the divine offer of immortality. Rather than regarding immortality as a natural property of soul,

Augustine's described it as the loving gift of the Good, who shed his own transcendence in order to break the powers of evil and death now trapping the soul. The incarnation of Christ was, to Augustine, an invitation for his soul to be united to his eternal source, an omnipresent God who knew him intimately and sought his return. Then his soul could become God by cleaving or adhering to him in a bond of love. As we discovered in Chapter 3, adhering to God in a bond of mutual love is the basis for immortality in Augustine. As Robert Wilken has pointed out: 'No other biblical word seemed to Augustine to embody the entire mystery of the faith so fully' (Wilken 2003: 72). In this sense Catholic Christianity was, above all else, a religion of personal immortality, one that was based on a God of personal love with whom the soul seeks to be united.

The whole of Augustine's thought is defined by a sense of plangent intimacy, of awareness of the deep presence of God tinged with sadness in the fallen soul. The need for the soul's return to God, its creator, dominates his theology. His soul had, he believed, a furtive understanding of a destiny beyond this life and a recognition of its incapacity to secure that life on its own. But God had become human so that Augustine might become divine. That was the conviction that drove his joint conversion to Catholicism and monasticism. Throughout his works, he describes the soul's absolute dependence upon God for salvation repeatedly and consistently. It is the lodestone of his Christianity. We have, he insists, no capacity to secure a life worth living beyond our physical existence without God's aid. Otherwise, we might be doomed not to extinction but to something worse, to an unending shadow life in agonizing separation from God. But our hope lies in a saviour who took on our condition in order to rescind it. Through the power of Christ, still present in his church, our souls may again be made translucent in the presence of God and then be reunited with him.

There were, of course, different theological accounts of these matters, even within the orthodox Christian spectrum. Augustine's is only one of these. His version puts considerable emphasis on the communal nature of this adherence to God. We saw this in both Chapters 2 and 3 when we looked at the heaven of heaven, the collection of souls that choose to contemplate the divine Wisdom without cessation. According to Augustine, therefore, community is the proper form of human immortality. He and Monica were given a glimpse of that reality at Ostia and it is to that community in union with God that he aspired to return. That process was often described in Eastern Christianity as 'deification'. Augustine rarely uses the equivalent Latin term, although recent scholarship has conclusively demonstrated he shares the same theological idea (Meconi 2013). In this respect he is part of the development of the Nicene tradition, drawing out its inner resources in light of the New Testament foundations upon which it rested. Augustine's thought on these matters is, therefore, a theological variation of the general patristic understanding of the nature and purpose of Christ, and the promise of human deification that his death and resurrection made possible. According to that tradition, immortality is not within the elemental nature of a divine soul. The soul lacks that autonomy as a creature of God and it cannot secure its salvation on its own power. It is only through the divine love, expressed through the incarnation of Christ, that the soul can be saved. And, for Augustine, the only true form of immortal salvation was union with God amid a community of souls restored to the divine presence.

The idea that humans are meant for union with God, indeed for deification, may sound like some religion other than Christianity. Indeed, that may be an accurate observation about much of popular Christianity today. On the ambient surface, Christianity often presents itself as being primarily about many other earthly matters. But ancient Christianity was different in its self-conception: it concentrated on creating a distinctive community that offered a new identity in communion with Christ. That meant a life by which the soul could be transformed ethically and come to express love and respect to others derived from the love manifested by the incarnate Christ. And so hope for a future life rested upon Christ, already manifest within the baptized soul, and in his shared presence within the ecclesial community. That helps us – as contemporary readers of Augustine – to make some sense of his emphasis on communion with God in this life. For Augustine believed, with intense conviction, that human life had meaning precisely to the extent that the soul was drawn into the reality of God. Here his depiction of God in the first account of his enlightenment – discussed in Chapter 1 – is worth recalling, 'Eternal truth, and true love, and beloved eternity: you are my God' (*Confessions* VII.10.16). God's rescue of the soul does not occur, as it were, on a level plain of existence, as one being to another. The saviour of the soul is the author of its life. That God is reality itself, absolute being. Nothing else could be relied upon, for that being would be a creature. Thus, God's perfection draws the soul to himself and his love alone can restore it.

That is a striking claim, one that was central to the orthodox Christianity Augustine adopted. It was not an abstract theory for Augustine, but the result of his failed efforts at moral self-improvement followed by the enlightenment experience that had transformed him. From the beginning of his writing as a Catholic, Augustine found this Christian conception of God utterly convincing. He came to believe that a struggle had been going on all his life, a tension within him between the feverous consciousness of a false self over against a new self. He was cured through the medicinal power of a divine physician who attended to him. Christ, the divine source of all reality, had been calling to him in the depth of the soul, the creator of the universe present to him as an individual. To contemporary ears accustomed at least to cultural fragments of Christianity – if only as riffs in gospel spirituals or the blues – Augustine's personal laments to God may seem familiar and unexceptional. But in the world of late antiquity, this idea of the ultimate God's intentional presence to the soul was a challenging claim. That was because the religious imagination of the ancients was still based on the older representation of the divine as quasi-physical, with a location in space and time. The novel conception of transcendence had not yet taken firm hold, leaving a lingering sense of spatial remoteness to the One God. This would have been true for pagans, including Platonists, who expected direct interaction to occur only with intermediary gods. The One of the Platonists, though omnipresent to the soul, did not interact with the soul directly nor did it engage the soul in a reciprocal association. This theological conception of intermediation was apparent as well in some forms of Christianity, such as Arianism – discussed in Chapter 1. For Arians, the Christ was an intermediary power, a creature produced by the ultimate God, the Father. But for Nicene Catholics like Augustine, the driving force of their religion was the complete divinity of Christ, the person of God who became incarnate. Belief in Christ meant, therefore, that God was totally present to the souls of believers through him. They were dealing directly with the transcendent God who was, nonetheless, attentive to them as human individuals. For Catholics like Augustine, the incarnation of Christ – understood as the true God from the true God – changed everything.

As a result, orthodox Christianity stood out to Augustine once he grasped its sophisticated balance between transcendence and immanence. As we have seen, he claimed not just to understand its conception of God, but to have had unmediated knowledge of God, his soul translucent in the intelligible light of divine Wisdom. That experience of Christian enlightenment initiated his story as a Christian; it did not end it. Once he had been baptized, the cure of his soul could begin in earnest, directed by Christ the physician of souls. Augustine explains that process in terms of what ancient Catholics called the 'whole Christ'. On this understanding of Christ, the incarnation was not a one-off event. Christ remains present within the souls of the members of the church. They form the body of Christ, the 'living soul of the faithful' (*Confessions* XIII.34.49). The incarnation thus is regarded as continuing with Christ as the head of the church and the faithful as his body. As Augustine says in *On the Epistle of John* I.2: 'The Word was made flesh and dwelled among us; the church is joined to that flesh, and Christ made whole, head and body.' This thinking had its basis in the Pauline conception of existing 'in Christ'. This does not mean that the Christian is identical with Christ, rather that the souls of the faithful are conjoined with Christ, adhering or cleaving to him.

The upshot of this line of reflection is that Augustine does not regard the soul's search for salvation to be an individual quest. It cannot be, to use a famous phrase of Plotinus from *Ennead* VI.9.11, 'the flight of the alone to the alone'. It must instead be a communal endeavour, so that Christ is understood to support the soul's journey through his presence in the church. Deification is therefore not a private process, but one rooted in the Christian community. This is so because the soul needs divine aid, and that is available from two ecclesial sources: the Bible and the sacraments. The sacramental life of the church sustains the soul's spiritual recovery, especially through baptism and the Eucharist. The latter was understood as immediate communion of the soul with Christ and the supreme expression of his presence within the community. Moreover the Word of God could be found still present and efficacious in the book of the church, the Bible. This, Augustine believed, is the primary medium by which Christ speaks to the soul and its verses have powerful curative effects for its moral condition. This point is evident on every page of the *Confessions,* which is saturated with biblical discourse. Here we need to grasp, however, that Augustine's refers not to purely literal readings of scripture, but to methods for searching the texts for deeper meanings. Those included symbolic, moral and allegorical readings meant to uncover a wealth of content not evident to a surface review. Moreover, biblical passages address the specific moral and spiritual ailments of the soul. A specific passage might snag on the rough moral edges of the soul and soften them. In this way, Christ cures the soul, something unavailable to a soul seeking God on its own. This is what grace is for Augustine, the divine aid that souls need to make their return to God. The whole Christ speaks to the soul through the book of the church and sustains the soul through its communal rituals. Nesting in the church, the soul is in union with Christ its saviour. The Christian self is, therefore, an ecclesial self, a soul formed by the whole Christ present in his church. Absent that communal source of grace, the soul is just a rolling stone.

# Beatitude

From his first writings after his enlightenment experiences in Milan, even before he was baptized, Augustine admitted his need for a power beyond himself to break the chains of his addictions. Christ, the divine Wisdom, did that for him, flooding his consciousness with a higher level of understanding and drawing his deepest self into union with the divine. But it was the larger Christ, the Christ present in the Christian community, who sustained those extraordinary moments through the church's prayer, observance and discipline. If that was true for him, Augustine concluded, it was true for everyone. Here lies another defining aspect of Catholic Christianity: it was accessible to people from all backgrounds and social levels. Within its ecclesial community, all earthly distinctions were meant to fall away.

Much has been written about the appeal of ancient Christianity in the deeply stratified society of the Roman Empire (Stark 1996). In the *Confessions,* Augustine explains that appeal in sharp contrast to the elitism of Manichaeism and, especially, Platonism. The latter was both culturally prestigious and a rival path to salvation. He knew very well that the Platonists in Rome claimed that their great teachers had achieved union with the One through the practice of the philosophical life. That was certainly not going to work for him, and, in his estimation, for most other people as well. There were several reasons for this. In his case, he had tried repeatedly to change his life on his own, to no avail, even after studying the methods of the Platonists. Moreover, philosophy was not a widely accessible way of life. To be a philosopher in antiquity required a lengthy and expensive education, available only to members of the wealthier classes. It also assumed a life of continued leisure, one that would allow the philosopher to lead a leisured life of contemplation. Augustine had indeed received an expensive liberal arts education, though his approach was pre-professional. His parents had borrowed the money to get him the education necessary to practice the rhetorical profession. He was never a true philosopher. What Augustine realized was that if philosophy was a path to salvation, it was an exceptionally elite one. To a Platonist this elitism may not have been ethically troubling, since their commitment to reincarnation helped to obviate the apparent injustice involved. Those fortunate souls, whose process of education through multiple reincarnations had prepared them for the final stage of contemplation, were born to the leisured class and had the means to become philosophers. But to Augustine this seemed implausible and restrictive. Moreover, many uneducated Christians, whose lives evinced conspicuous sanctity, seemed to merit salvation despite their humble origins and limited learning.

There is a remarkable passage on the scope of Platonism in *On True Religion,* one of the first works written just after he returned to North Africa and took up the monastic life. There he imagines Plato to be alive and to be engaged in dialectic with a disciple. First, Augustine succinctly summarizes Plato's teaching: The pure mind can discover immaterial truth if it is healed and freed from materiality. That immaterial world was made by an eternal God and the rational soul can contemplate it. Now the disciple asks: What if there were a teacher who could convince the multitude of people of the truth of Plato's theory? Would that man not be great and divine? Plato then replies that such a man would need to be illumined from birth by God and strengthened against the wicked who would oppose his teaching. Then this divine man, the incarnate wisdom of God, would be able to convert humanity to the truth of transcendentalism. Augustine then concludes that this has, in fact, happened. While Platonism had not accomplished the conversion of humanity, Christianity has now done so, for the Wisdom of God has indeed been present in a man on behalf of our salvation. In consequence, that divine wisdom is available to all humans, both those who can understand the depths of its teachings and those who can only believe what is beyond their educational level or capacity. Thus, in contrast to Platonism, Christianity is the religion that has brought beatitude to all humanity.

Monica was the chief witness of the scope and power of Christianity. She is featured from the first works Augustine wrote, as well as throughout the *Confessions*, where he sketches out her biography in book IX. An uneducated woman, Monica is the source of conclusive wisdom to the educated male interlocutors who surround Augustine in his seminar and the sole person to whom her son defers to in *On the Happy Life* (3). Augustine praises her for grasping hold of the 'treasury of philosophy', something that she acquired from the divine font of wisdom itself. Most important was her interior ascension at Ostia, where she attained union with the divine Wisdom in exactly the same degree as her learned son (*On the Happy Life* 1.10). She is, therefore, a living counterexample to the claim that true wisdom is available only to philosophers. Hers was a wisdom born of sanctity, a divine gift. As such she was proof of the transformative power of Christianity available beyond the confines of the intellectual elites.

This spiritual egalitarianism is a powerful theme in Augustine's conversion narrative. It contributed to his expansion of contemplation beyond the restricted philosophical model. He came instead to see Christian contemplation as grounded in the interpretation of scripture and in the divine grace that this practice could help impart to the soul. This can be seen in the description of interior contemplation that he gives in the first treatise he wrote as a member of the clergy, *On the Usefulness of Believing*. Here Augustine underscores the importance of faith, which he explains as adopting the Christian life, living in accord with its precepts, and looking at the world through the lens of its spiritual teachings. Faith is not a cognitive leap in the absence of adequate evidence – which is often our contemporary definition. Instead, it is an integral way of life through which the soul comes to discover and deepen its relationship with God. That alone can help to reorient the soul and bring it to a level where its cognitive functions are no longer occluded by the passions. This should remind us that behind Augustine's egalitarianism lies his judgement of the fallen condition of humanity. All humans are fallen and in need of rehabilitation under divine guidance. None has a divine of soul or a ruined fragment of spirit within itself. Thus, the universality of the fall supports the need for a life of faith, one that can deepen into Christian contemplation of God.

For these reasons, Augustine came to centre the practice of contemplation in a specifically Christian form of life based on beatitudes. Those powerful precepts from the Sermon on the Mount (Mt. 5.3-10) were understood as stages in the soul's ascension to God. This ascension through the beatitudes can be found in a treatise entitled *On the Lord's Sermon on the Mount*, also written around 393 just after his ordination as a Catholic presbyter. Here are the eight stages:

1  The soul begins its ascent with humility and in renunciation of its spiritual pride. It must recognize that its fallen state precludes knowledge of the divine unless it seeks a cure. That can be found only in the scriptures and in the teachings of the church that can guide the soul. The soul must also become aware of the stakes involved, for its spiritual state will one day be judged by God. Once it has humbly put aside its mistaken belief in its own capacities, it can begin its ascent.

2  At the next stage, the soul turns to the reading of scripture. By meditation upon its deeper meaning, the soul can begin to be cured of the passions that afflict it. Augustine regards this as a practice necessary for both the unlearned and learned alike.

3  Next the soul, through the medicinal effects of scripture, can recognize its fallen state. Now confessional introspection is possible as the soul recognizes the habits of sin that dominate it. Its consciousness, previously entrapped by sinful desires, can begin to overcome its fallen condition. It is at this stage that the soul can also come to estimate the extent of its estrangement from its divine source.

4  The soul now struggles as it tries to free itself from the 'destructive sweetness' of its sinful desires. That lethal sweetness must be faced with fortitude, and the soul

must hunger and thirst for freedom from those delights. Augustine puts this succinctly: 'What is held fast in delight is not relinquished without sorrow.'

5 This is the stage at which the support of the Christian community comes into play. A spiritual director is necessary to advise the soul on how to extricate itself. This is an act of mercy, whereby the wisdom of the Christian community can be leveraged to assist the soul to break chains of its addictions.

6 At last the soul achieves purity of heart, the spiritual level stipulated by the beatitudes as necessary to see God. The soul has begun to engage in good works for others and is no longer centred on itself. It is able to be serene and to engage in interior contemplation of the highest good. The soul's likeness to God is beginning to be restored, and its warring elements are coming into harmony.

7 The seventh level is the completion of the ascent. The soul contemplates truth and comes into the presence of divine wisdom itself. Its likeness to God is fully restored and the whole self is at peace. This is the meaning of 'blessed are the peacemakers, for they shall be called children of God'.

8 Augustine adds a final eighth stage in which the soul goes back to stage 1 and starts over. This is a surprising but characteristic Augustinian move, underscoring the still fallen condition of all souls while still embodied, even those like himself who have enjoyed contemplative union with God. There is no secure stage of enlightenment for the Augustinian Christian, only the prospect of continuing exercise of the beatitudes. For no soul is wholly settled spiritually and beyond the possibility of sin, even if the soul has been restored to its likeness to God through interior contemplation.

This was Monica's path to the vision at Ostia. Hers was the accomplishment of beatitude through divine grace and she served as a paradigm of that universal possibility to all humanity. That was the teaching of the Catholic – that is 'universal' – Church that drew Augustine, even to the extent that it could include someone with his past.

# Contemplative Christianity

'What else is the face of God than the truth itself for which we sigh and to which, as the object of our love, we are restoring ourselves as pure and beautiful?' (*On Order* 1.8.23). To see the face of God was the goal of the religion of Augustine (Wilken 2003). The incarnation of Christ, the divine wisdom itself, had offered to humanity not just an opening to life beyond death, but to the only immortality really worth having – communion with God. Through communion with Christ, Augustine believed that humanity could secure something more worthy than just reincarnation or shadowy subsistence in the underworld. The soul could attain everlasting life in the presence of the eternal and infinite God, the creator of finite reality. All this we can know, not just guess at, by following a way of life taught to us by Christ the divine teacher and sustained for us by Christ the physician of souls.

These were the core credenda of orthodox Christianity that Augustine found so compelling in 386, what he believed had been revealed to him when his soul 'touched' divine wisdom. And these are the elements that seemed most salient to him about orthodox Christianity, making it rise above the other options in the crowded religious marketplace of late antiquity. They became the staples of his preaching over decades as bishop in Hippo Regius repeated time and again in extemporaneous sermons to his North African congregation – hundreds of which were preserved by scribes and still extant today. He taught a Christian way of life that would lead to beatitude and thence to communion with God, sometimes fleetingly in this life but perpetually in the next. It was, in consequence, a contemplative religion. Its efforts at communal exercises of charity, for which it was renowned in the ancient pagan world, and its commendation of a moderate personal ethic, were meant to direct souls to follow Christ, the good shepherd, into reunion with the divine Father. In these efforts to understand, expound and shape orthodox Christianity, Augustine was not alone. Indeed, he was a member of the greatest generation of Christian thinkers since the evangelists, the founders and expositors of the Nicene tradition. He was a contemporary of Athanasius of Alexandria, Ambrose of Milan, Jerome, Basil of Caesarea, Gregory Nazianzen and Gregory of Nyssa, among others. All were defining figures in the development of orthodox Christianity both in the Greek East and the Latin West. While each had unique aspects to his thinking, they shared a common account of Christianity with Augustine. As we conclude this excavatory essay into the layered deposits of that age, we might review several of its constitutive elements.

The God of Nicene Christianity was a transcendent God. As we discovered, Augustine wanted no part of popular North Africa Christianity in his early years because it was too crudely anthropomorphic in its interpretation of the Bible. But the God of Catholic Christianity, as articulated by sophisticated thinkers like Ambrose, was different for two reasons. First, it was evident that the scriptures had been understood since apostolic times to contain numerous levels of meaning, a practice that blunted literalist critics. Moreover, God was clearly understood to be transcendent of space, time and the physical universe. That philosophically advanced representation of God dovetailed with the search for higher meanings in scripture. The result was a powerful religious alloy. Otherwise, Christianity would have seemed to be just another cosmic cult, with an ascending and descending redeemer who disappeared into the clouds on his way to his father out in the heavens, promising to return in the same way. There were other religions much like it around. But Catholic Christianity was not about space travel for its redeemer or for the souls of its adherents. It was about something unimaginably deeper and more profound: a God who was infinite being itself and who had nonetheless become human to effect the salvations of souls. That was the counter-intuitive message of this new religion, a radical departure fusing elements of religion and philosophy already in solution in late antiquity. It grabbed the imaginations of so many great thinkers of the age, making transcendence ineluctable and immortality accessible.

It made God transparent as well. No more remote mountaintop eyries like Olympus or Sinai, no more hidden places on the edge of the heavens. God was nowhere and everywhere in a different way; neither in space nor in time, but omnipresent spiritually. The way to God was no longer out and up but down and within. And so God was closer to the soul than ever before. And there was no way to escape him, something that seems at times a bit terrifying in the *Confessions,* as Augustine recounts coming to adjust to such complete divine proximity. But accessing God was now no longer a problem. He was there within the soul, accessible whenever one wished – something the *Confessions* models on every page.

The religion of orthodox Christianity was, therefore, centred on the practice of the presence of God, sustained by his collective presence in those souls who make up the pilgrim church on earth, and who live in communion with Christ. As a result, there is a tensile strength to be found in the balance between God's transcendence and immanence. What can never be lost sight of in Augustine is that he did not simply propose theories about a transcendent God, in a fashion that ignored the presence of God within the soul. Discursive theology served to direct the soul towards God. Any representation that would attempt to capture God accurately from afar would only reinforce the soul's distance. That was the balance in Augustine's thought, finding ways to speak of God through scripture and reason that guide the soul without the failure of misplaced objectivity.

Yet, the God of Augustine may seem like a strange God today, when viewed across the centuries. Perhaps this is because those aspects that once made his contemplative Christianity so compelling in late antiquity have long since been assimilated into the religious vernacular, such as the idea of divine transcendence itself. Yet that very strangeness may have its appeal. Reading Augustine can give the shock of encountering ancient Christianity in the age of its orthodox coalescence, allowing us to see its original shape and form. In doing so we can discern in Augustine a rich understanding of God: A God who is beyond our finite categories of thought, and yet a God who has revealed himself in the language of the scriptures in order to offer us icons that unite our souls with him. Augustine was, as we have found, no literalist in his reading of the Bible, and his understanding of God began with anthropomorphic images but it did not end there. God should not be conceived as a finite person, nor even as a perfect being. And God should not be reduced to an agent who acts in time or across space. Those biblical images have their uses, in his view, but they can also lead to confusion and distortion when they harden into theology. This is especially true of divine volition, which should not be represented as being exercised in time, even if it appears as such to us. God is not a finite agent whose omnipotent will is temporal. That mistake emerges from a materialistic conception of God, one that fails to understand the fundamentally transcendent and eternal nature of the One God. But Augustine's God is true being, perfect love and total power, existing in eternity and loading into the history of a fallen world. Our existence through time is, therefore, God's goodness expressed in the continuing sequence of creation that is earthly life. To lose that dimension of contemplative depth is to foreshorten Augustine's immense vision of God.

That point should remind us that one striking characteristic of the thought of Augustine and his Nicene contemporaries was the integration of philosophy, theology and spiritual practices – to use contemporary terms. The great divorce of philosophy from theology and their emergence as academic disciplines was a product of the medieval age and the rise of the universities. That fissure brought with it the separation of both philosophy and theology from the contemplative practices that were so integral to Augustine. As we look back to Augustine, we need to reassemble these components – philosophy, theology and spirituality – if we are to understand ancient contemplative Christianity. This inquiry has been an essay in that restoration, in a return to the sources of Western Christianity, and to the recovery of its original meaning as articulated by its greatest ancient expositor.

# Bibliography

## Selected Works of Augustine

*Early Works*

Burleigh, J. H. S. 1953. *Augustine: Earlier Writings*. Philadelphia: The Westminster Press

McMahon, J. J., et al. 2002. *The Fathers of the Church*. vol. 4. Washington DC: The Catholic University of America Press.

Ramsey, B. 2000. *The Works of Saint Augustine: Soliloquies*. Hyde Park, NY: New City Press.

Schopp, L. et al. 2008. *The Fathers of the Church*. vol. 5. Washington DC: The Catholic University of America Press.

*Confessions:*

Boulding, M. 2001. *The Confessions*. Hyde Park, NY: New City Press.

Chadwick, H. 1991. *Confessions*. Oxford and New York: Oxford University Press.

*On The Trinity:*

Rotelle, J. E. 2012. *The Works of Saint Augustine: The Trinity*. Hyde Park, NY: New City Press.

*City of God*

Bettenson, H. 2003. *St. Augustine: Concerning the City of God against the Pagans*. London: Penguin Books.

Ramsey, B. ed. 2000. *The Works of Saint Augustine: The City of God*. vols. 1 & 2. Hyde Park, NY: New City Press.

## Letters

Ramsey, B. [2001] 2005. *The Works of Saint Augustine: Letters*, vols. 1–4. Hyde Park, NY: New City Press.

## Sermons

Ramsey, B. ed. 2007. *The Works of Saint Augustine: Essential Sermons.* Hyde Park, NY: New City Press.

## Reconsiderations

Bogan, M. I. 1968. *Saint Augustine: The Retractations.* Washington DC: The Catholic University of America Press.

# Ancient Authors

## Celsus

Hoffman, R. 1987. *Celsus on the True Doctrine: A Discourse against the Christians.* New York: Oxford University Press.

## Justin Martyr

Falls, T. B. 2008. *The Fathers of the Church: Writings of Saint Justin Martyr.* Washington DC: The Catholic University of America Press.

## Plato

Cooper, J. M. 1997. *Plato: Complete Works.* Indianapolis: Hackett Publishing

## Plotinus

Armstrong, A. H. 1966–88. *Plotinus I-VII.* Cambridge, MA: Harvard University Press.

MacKenna, S. 1991. *Plotinus: The Enneads.* London: Penguin Books.

*Porphyry*

Armstrong, A. H. 1966. 'Life of Plotinus', in *Plotinus* I. Cambridge, MA: Harvard University Press.

Hoffman, R. 1994. *Porphyry's against the Christians: The Literary Remains*. New York: Prometheus Press.

# Modern Scholarship

Armstrong, A. H. 1966–88. *Plotinus I-VII*. Cambridge, MA: Harvard University Press.

Armstrong, A. H. 1979. *Plotinian and Christian Studies*. London: Variorum Reprints.

Armstrong, A. H. ed. 1986. *Classical Mediterranean Spirituality: Egyptian, Greek, Roman*. New York: Crossroads Press.

Armstrong, A. H. 1990. *Hellenic and Christian Studies*. London: Variorum Reprints.

Athanassiadi, P. and Frede, M. eds. 1999. *Pagan Monotheism in Late Antiquity*. Oxford: Clarendon Press.

Brown, P. 1967/2000. *Augustine of Hippo: A Biography*. Berkeley CA: University of California Press.

Cameron, M. 2012. *Christ Meets Me Everywhere: Augustine's Early Figurative Exegesis*. Oxford: Oxford University Press.

Cherniss, H. 1965. 'The Philosophical Economy of the Theory of Ideas'. In *Studies in Plato's Metaphysics*. Edited by R. E. Allen, 1–12. London: Humanities Press.

Evans, G. R. 1982. *Augustine on Evil*. Cambridge: Cambridge University Press.

Gerson, L. P. 2013. *From Plato to Platonism*. Ithaca: Cornell University Press.

Gerson, L. P. 2017. 'Platonism Versus Naturalism.' In *Defining Platonism*. Edited by John F. Finnamore and Sarah Klitenic Ware. Steubenville, OH: Franciscan University Press.

Hadot, P. 1995. *Philosophy as a Way of Life*. Oxford: Blackwell.

Hadot, P. 2002. *What Is Ancient Philosophy?* Cambridge MA: Harvard University Press.

Hadot, P. 2011. *The Present Alone Is Our Happiness*. Stanford: Stanford University Press.

Harmless, W. S. J. 2010. *Augustine in His Own Words*. Washington DC: The Catholic University of America Press.

Harmless, W. S. J. 2014. *Augustine and the Mystery of the Human* Heart. Unpublished manuscript.

Harrison, C. 1992. *Beauty and Revelation in the Thought of Saint Augustine*. Oxford: Clarendon.

Harrison, C. 2000. *Christian Truth and Fractured Humanity: Augustine in Context*. Oxford: Oxford University Press.

Harrison, C. 2006. *Rethinking Augustine's Early Theology: An Argument for Continuity*. Oxford: Oxford University Press.

Headley, D. 2008. *Living Forms of the Imagination*. London: Continuum

Headley, D. 2016. *The Iconic Imagination*. London: Bloomsbury

Hick, J. 1966. *Evil and the God of Love*. New York: Harper and Row.

Hollingworth, M. 2013. *Saint Augustine of Hippo: An Intellectual Biography*. Oxford: Oxford University Press.

Kenney, J. P. 1986. 'Monotheistic and Polytheistic Elements in Classical Mediterranean Spirituality'. In *Classical Mediterranean Spirituality*. Edited by A. H. Armstrong. New York: Crossroad Press.

Kenney, J. P. 1991. *Mystical Monotheism: A Study in Ancient Platonic Theology*. Hanover, NH: Brown University Press.

Kenney, J. P. 2005. *The Mysticism of Saint Augustine: Rereading the Confessions*. London and New York: Routledge.

Kenney, J. P. 2006. 'Commentary on Stern-Gillet'. *Proceedings of the Boston Area Colloquium in Ancient Philosophy*, XXII.

Kenney, J. P. 2013. *Contemplation and Classical Christianity: A Study in Augustine*. Oxford: Oxford University Press.

King, K. 2005. *What Is Gnosticism?* Cambridge MA: Harvard University Press.

Kolbet, P. 2010. *Augustine and the Cure of Souls*. Notre Dame, IN: Notre Dame University Press.

Lane Fox, R. 2015. *Augustine: Conversions to Confessions*. New York: Basic Books.

Louth, A. 1981. *The Origins of the Christian Mystical Tradition from Plato to Denys*. Oxford: Oxford University Press.

MacMullen, R. 1981. *Paganism in the Roman Empire*. New Haven: Yale University Press.

Markus, R. A. 1970. *Saeculum: History and Society in the Theology of Saint Augustine*. Cambridge: Cambridge University Press.

Markus, R. A. 1990. *The End of Ancient Christianity*. Cambridge: Cambridge University Press.

Mathewes, Charles. T. 2001. *Evil and the Augustinian Tradition*. Cambridge: Cambridge University Press.

McGinn, B. 1991. *The Presence of God: A History of Western Christian Mysticism*. vol. 1. New York: Crossroads Press.

Meconi, D. V. S. J. 2013. *The One Christ: St. Augustine's Theology of Deification*. Washington DC: The Catholic University of America Press.

Mitchell, S. and van Nuffelen, P. 2010 *One God: Pagan Monotheism in the Roman Empire*. Cambridge: Cambridge University Press.

Nussbaum, Martha. 2003. *Upheavals of Thought: The Intelligence of Emotion*. Cambridge: Cambridge University Press.

O'Connell, R. J. 1968. *St. Augustine's Early Theory of Man, A.D. 386-391*. Cambridge MA: Harvard University Press.

O'Connell, R. J. 1969. *St. Augustine's Confessions: The Odyssey of Soul*. Cambridge, MA: Harvard University Press.

O'Connell, R. J. 1987. *The Origin of the Soul in St. Augustine's Later Works*. New York: Fordham University Press.

O'Connell, R. J. 1996. *Images of Conversion in St. Augustine's Confessions*. New York: Fordham University Press.

O'Daly, G. J. P. 1987. *Augustine's Philosophy of Mind*. London: Duckworth.

O'Donnell, J. 1992. *The Confessions of Augustine*. Oxford: Oxford University Press.

O'Donnell, J. J. 2005. *Augustine: A New Biography*. New York: HarperCollins.

Remes, P. 2007. *Plotinus on Self: The Philosophy of the 'We'*. Cambridge: Cambridge University Press.

Remes, P. 2008. *Neoplatonism*. Berkeley: University of California Press.

Reeve, C. D. C. 1988. *Philosopher-Kings: The Argument of Plato's Republic*. Princeton: Princeton University Press.

Reeve, C. D. C. 2013. *Blindness and Reorientation: Problems in Plato's Republic*. Oxford: Oxford University Press

Rist, J. M. 1994. *Augustine: Ancient Thought Baptized*. Cambridge: Cambridge University Press.

Rombs, R. 2006. *Saint Augustine and the Fall of the Soul*. Washington DC: The Catholic University of America.

Ryle, G. 1949. *The Concept of Mind*. New York: Barnes and Noble.

Siedentop, L. 2014. *Inventing the Individual*. Cambridge, MA: Harvard University Press.

Sorabji, R. 2006. *Self: Ancient and Modern Insights about Individuality, Life, and Death*. Chicago: University of Chicago Press.

Stark, R. 1996. *The Rise of Christianity*. Princeton: Princeton University Press.

Stern-Gillet, Suzanne. 2006. 'Consciousness and Introspection in Plotinus and Augustine'. *Proceedings of the Boston Area Colloquium in Ancient Philosophy*, XXII.

Stock, Brian. 1998. *Augustine the Reader: Meditation, Self-knowledge and the Ethics of Interpretation*. Cambridge, MA: Harvard University Press.

Strousma, G. 2008. *The End of Sacrifice: Religious Transformations in Late Antiquity*. Chicago: The University of Chicago Press.

Strousma, G. 2016. *The Scriptural Universe of Ancient Christianity*. Cambridge, MA: Harvard University Press.

Surin, K. 1986. *Theology and the Problem of Evil*. Oxford: Basil Blackwell.

Taylor, C. 1989. *Sources of the Self: The Making of the Modern Identity*. Cambridge, MA: Harvard University Press.

Teske, R. J. 2008. *To Know God and the Soul: Essays on the Thought of Saint Augustine*. Washington DC: The Catholic University of America Press.

Tilley, T. 1991. *The Evils of Theodicy*. Washington DC: Georgetown University Press.

Turner, D. 1995. *The Darkness of God: Negativity in Christian Mysticism*. Cambridge: Cambridge University Press.

van Geest, P. 2011. *The Incomprehensibility of God: Augustine as a Negative Theologian*. Leuven: Peeters Press.

Wetzel, J. 1992. *Augustine and the Limits of Virtue*. Cambridge: Cambridge University Press.

Wilken, R. L. 2003. *The Spirit of Early Christian Thought*. New Haven: Yale University Press.

Williams, R. 2016. *On Augustine*. London: Bloomsbury.

Zum Brunn, E. 1988. *St. Augustine: Being and Nothingness*. New York: Paragon House.

# INDEX